Broken

(in the best possible way)

Broken

(in the best possible way)

....

Jenny Lawson

FULL-GROWN MAMMAL

Henry Holt and Company

New York

Henry Holt and Company

Publishers since 1866

120 Broadway

New York, New York 10271

www.henryholt.com

Library of Congress Cataloging-in-Publication Data

Names: Lawson, Jenny, 1973– author.

Title: Broken (in the best possible way) / Jenny Lawson.

Description: First edition. | New York : Henry Holt and Company, 2021.

Identifiers: LCCN 2020013954 (print) | LCCN 2020013955 (ebook) |

ISBN 9781250077035 (hardcover) | ISBN 9781250077059 (ebook) |

9781250799265 (international edition)

Subjects: LCSH: Lawson, Jenny, 1973– | Lawson, Jenny, 1973—Mental health. |

Journalists—United States—Biography. | Humorists, American—

21st century—Biography. | Mental illness—Humor.

Classification: LCC PN4874.L285 A3 2021 (print) |

LCC PN4874.L285 (ebook) | DDC 070.92—dc23

LC record available at https://lccn.loc.gov/2020013954

LC ebook record available at https://lccn.loc.gov/2020013955

Our books may be purchased in bulk for promotional, educational, or business use.
Please contact your local bookseller or the Macmillan Corporate and
Premium Sales Department at (800) 221-7945, extension 5442,
or by e-mail at MacmillanSpecialMarkets@macmillan.com.

First U.S. Edition 2021

Endpaper illustration by Omar Rayyan

Case stamp illustration by Denise Kendig

Designed by Michelle McMillian

Printed in the United States of America

1   3   5   7   9   10   8   6   4   2

Dedicated to my husband,
without whom this book would not exist.
Mainly because he would not quit yelling
at me to stop binge-watching Netflix
and get some fucking work done.

But also because he's funnier than I am in person,
gives me incredible material, and loves me
even when I don't always love myself.
Thanks, mister.

Ring the bells that still can ring.
Forget your perfect offering.
There is a crack in everything.
That's how the light gets in.

—LEONARD COHEN

Contents

Broken

(in the best possible way)

Jenny Lawson, Full-Grown Mammal:
An Introduction

You probably just picked up this book thinking, *What the shit is this all about?* And frankly I'm right there with you. Honestly, I just got here myself. By the time you read this it will be an actual, fully formed, and probably horribly offensive book, but at the moment I'm writing this it's just a bunch of sentences, paralyzing anxiety, and a lot of angst. Some people write a book a week, but I'm achingly slow and filled with self-doubt and writer's block, so by the time you read this I will have gone through years of "WRITING IS SO LONELY AND I HATE EVERYTHING AND EVERYONE." I will have gone through the writing period when I tell my husband that real writers write drunk and edit sober, and then later the editing period when I tell him I have edited this notion and have to write drunk and also edit drunk, and even the period where I just lock myself in a room and force myself to write and it's glorious and beautiful until I wake up the next day and realize it's garbage and delete everything.

You, on the other hand, will only see the finished product. Shiny and edited and pasted together with the tears of copy editors whom I have sent to an early grave and/or multiple bars. Will it be worth it? No damn idea. But I can't stop, because writers write always. Not *well*, necessarily. But they write. And you are a reader. So you read. (Unless you are listening to the audiobook, in which case, I guess you are a hearer? Is that right? That seems like the wrong word but I can't think of the correct one right now. But I bet you're a great hearer, even if that word doesn't exist.) I don't even know you and I can tell you're special. Mostly because everyone seems special to me. Granted, some of that is because I have avoidant personality disorder and imposter syndrome, which automatically makes me think everyone in the world is better than me, and some of it is because you're still reading this (or hearering it) even though it's pretty obvious that I'm stalling because I'm not sure what to write about; I appreciate that and I owe you a drink.

(OH! "LISTENING TO." Those are the words I was looking for. Not "hearering." Although I sort of like the melody of the word "hearering" now, so let's keep it.)

This whole introduction is a pretty good indication of the baffling wordsmithery that you can expect here, and that's a good thing because 1) now you've been warned, so you can't blame me if you hate this book, and 2) you're going to feel *so* much better about yourself in comparison.

I'm not just saying that to flatter you. Truly. I have managed to fuck shit up in shockingly impressive ways and still be considered a fairly acceptable person. In some ways I've actually made it my living. And because I'm so good at being publicly terrible, other people feel comfortable telling me about how awful they are at being an adult, and then I try to top them with a "Oh, you think that's bad?

Let me tell you how I tried to rescue a decapitated human head from my work," and then they're like, "Nah. HOLD MY BEER," and in the end I end up with a new best friend because *how could you not* love a person who couldn't understand where those terrible farting noises were coming from on the bus but then she realized that they were the noises of the dog toy in her purse that she was leaning on and everyone looked at her and so she ended up shaking a rubber foot at them while yelling, "I'M NOT FARTING. IT'S MY DOG'S FOOT." Answer: You can't. YOU LOVE THEM. Hard.

It's weird because we often try to present our fake, shiny, happy selves to others and make sure we're not wearing too-obvious pajamas at the grocery store, but really, who wants to see that level of fraud? No one. What we really want is to know we're not alone in our terribleness. We want to appreciate the failure that makes us perfectly us and wonderfully relatable to every other person out there who is also pretending that they have their shit together and didn't just eat that onion ring that fell on the floor. Human foibles are what make us *us*, and the art of mortification is what brings us all together.

A lot of people read my books because they love to laugh about all the terrible things you maybe shouldn't laugh at. I hope you find this book just as funny, but there's some really serious and raw stuff in here too, mostly related to my battles with mental illness. If I could choose the themes of my life, I assure you this book would be all about my successful otter rescue and how I became a sexy vampire who isn't allergic to dairy. But we don't get to pick who we are. I am still as broken as I was before, but with better stories and a little more insight into just how fucked up I am.

Even the title for this introduction comes from a conversation I had with a friend where we tried to win "worst at adulting." I pointed out that I could barely even be human and that at most I was just a full-grown mammal. But then I remembered that the thing that makes you a mammal is laying live young instead of eggs and lactating, but I couldn't even lactate properly. But then I remembered that men don't lay live young and they're still mammals, and I thought maybe I needed to consult a science book because I'd fucked up the definition, or that maybe it was another situation where men just get a pass because of that whole "I own a penis" thing, and then my friend was like, "I don't think you're supposed to say that you 'lay' live young," and I was like, "Yeah. Poor phrasing on my part. But in my defense, *I can't even mammal correctly*," and she refused to accept that and insisted that I recognize my accomplishments. "You are Jenny Lawson, full-grown mammal!" she said encouragingly and with confidence, and I said, "I think you just came up with my next book title," and she was like, "I think you could do better," but GUESS WHAT? I CAN'T AND NOW I FEEL BAD AGAIN.

But fuck that. Fuck feeling bad about eating floor onion rings. Fuck the shame that comes from wearing your clothes to bed so you're technically never (or always) in your pajamas. Fuck the people who make you feel bad for glorifying the odd behavior and questionable decisions that make you who you are. Those things are perfectly acceptable.

Be good. Be kind. Love each other. Fuck everything else. The only thing that matters is how you feel and how you've made others feel. And I feel okay (for the moment), and I make others feel okay by being a barometer of awkwardness and self-doubt.

I am Jenny Lawson, **full-grown mammal.**

And I am ready to begin.

I Already Forgot I Wrote This

I don't remember the first time I noticed I was losing my memory. This sounds like a joke but I only laughed when I read it again and realized how ridiculous it sounds. Extremely ridiculous, but to many of you who are nodding in agreement at what you just read, it's also extremely true. Also, now I'll have to remind half of you why you were nodding, and it's because I was talking about memory loss. And if you looked back at the first sentence to verify that that's what you were agreeing with because you didn't trust that that's what we were talking about, then you already know my pain.

I can blame some of this on my ADD, which gives me the attention level of a kitten on cocaine. One minute I'm having a brilliant thought (like wondering if flat-chested women ever get that sweaty underboob smell even if they don't have underboob), and then I suddenly find myself standing in front of an open refrigerator and thinking, *Why am I here?* But not like *Why am I here, and what is the purpose of life?* More like *Why am I in the kitchen? How did I get here? Why is there milk in this fridge if I'm lactose intolerant? WHOSE HOUSE IS THIS?* And then I remember that other people live with me, and that *they* probably bought the milk, but then I think, *Does milk always look that color? How do I know if it's gone bad?* and then I look for the expiration date on the jug and it says it's "good through November" but it doesn't have a year so I don't know if it's November of this year or last year so I end up standing there at the fridge in confusion, holding the milk in my hand, wondering if it's either very fresh or completely poisonous, and then Victor walks in and says, "Close the damn fridge. And why are you holding the milk? *You don't even drink milk,*" and I say, "What year is this?" and he looks at me as if I've lost my mind. Probably because he doesn't realize that I'm really asking what year the milk is from, not what year we're currently living in. Except then I start to wonder what year it is because I've gotten that wrong before. Then he gives me one of those concerned, irritated looks, but mostly because I'm letting all the cold air out of the refrigerator and less because he thinks I figured out time travel and I'm Jenny from the future who just returned from some sort of time loop where I killed someone who was worse than Hitler but who you don't know about because I killed him (which would be *my* first thought if someone asked me what year it was *because I give people the benefit of the doubt, Victor*). And also a little because he thinks I'm losing my mind. Mostly the fridge thing though, because he's used to the latter. If I'm being honest though, that confused irritation is probably one of the most stable parts of our relationship, and I think if I suddenly started to make sense now he'd suspect I'd been abducted by aliens.

Which—now that I think about it—I might have been, because the alien theory would account for all this missing time I've lost. It would explain all the times I find myself in the closet thinking,

Why am I here and who bought all these shoes? Or panickedly telling Victor that I can't find my phone while I'm actually talking to him on it. Victor says it wouldn't explain that last part, but *you don't know what aliens do, Victor.* They're unpredictable. Probably. I don't really remember. WHICH PROVES MY POINT.

Or! Maybe I'm a bunch of me's all living in different time dimensions and slipping forward and back, either with too much information to sound sane or missing vital information I should totally have.

It's not just small things I've forgotten. When I was younger I worried that my memory lapses were a sign I was blacking out terrible things and that one day I'd remember the terrible things that had been done to me in cults I'd obviously forgotten about and may have even started myself, but it's not that. I just have holes in my memory. I have forgotten entire vacations. I've forgotten countries I say I'd like to see, and then Victor will pull out pictures that show me in them. I remember the photograph. I remember the chicken running around in the background and the fact that Victor was trying to find the Spanish word for butter but called it something else. But everything outside of that picture is fog. And this is why I write. Because my mind is tricksy and unpredictable, and without pictures and stories and constant remembrances sometimes things slip away. And I slip away with them. I wonder where I go. Is there a part of me left behind forever on deserted beaches Victor insists I've slept on? Is another me forever seeing the moments of my life I seem to have forgotten?

It's not all bad. There are some perks to having a poor memory. I am eternally telling Victor that I found a great documentary we should watch about serial killers, only for him to stare at me in disbelief and remind me that we just watched it six months ago. Then I'll tell him he's insane and I'll watch it, angrily, as I'm certain he's just saying that because he wants to watch NASCAR, but then halfway through something will seem familiar and I'll realize he's right. Then six months later I'll tell him about a great documentary on serial killers I recorded for us and he'll stare at me and tell me that not only have I seen it multiple times, we've argued about whether I've seen it, and then I look at him like he's gone insane because I *DEFI-NITELY* have not seen this documentary and so I say, "YOU CAN JUST SAY YOU DON'T WANT TO WATCH IT. YOU DON'T HAVE TO GASLIGHT ME," but then I watch it again and at that same place I remember that I have seen it before and I also remember that this was the same place in the film I remembered I'd seen it before the last time I forgot that I'd watched it. And then I'm forced to tell Victor that he might be right, but I still finish it because I don't remember how it ends. And that's nice because I always have something new to watch.

It's the same with books. Even the ones I've read over and over are new to me toward the end. I can never remember if the butler did it or if Alice will escape Wonderland. I thought I was a big fan of Agatha Christie but it turns out I just read *Murder on the Orient Express* over and over, and each time I was a little disappointed in her because I usually figured out who did it before the end, but probably just because I'd read the same story a thousand times. It's worse when I use an e-reader because I try to buy books and my e-reader is like, "You already own that, dumbass," and I'm like, "Nuh-uh," and then it downloads and I see that I've highlighted parts of the book that I would totally highlight if it was me and read strange notes I've written in the pages. Some people might find this unsettling, and in some ways it is, but it's also sort of nice to always have a new book that I discuss with my book club (who is basically all of the me's who've read the book before and left weird notes in the edges). That sounds insane, but my book club is awesome and is possibly the largest group of people I encounter (even if all of them are me's that I've forgotten). They're very entertaining though, and when I read their notes I'll cry out, "YES! I AGREE SO MUCH! . . . I THOUGHT IT WAS JUST ME." And I guess that makes sense because it is just me, since I'm the one who wrote them, but still, it's reassuring, and after I forget that I've read a book multiple times it provides a much-needed comfort.

There are advantages to having a spotty memory, the biggest being that it has kept me married for more than twenty years. I'll have fights with Victor and I'll be very angry over something terrible he's done, but it's not unusual for me to forget what it was we were fighting about *while still fighting*, which makes it very hard to win even though I know I'm right and that he should just trust me and apologize and maybe buy me a ferret. Victor remembers every word, so I'm forever reminding myself to buy a tape recorder to record the fight so I can stop and refresh myself, but I never remember to do that, and in fact as I'm writing this I just remembered that tape recorders probably don't even exist anymore as I haven't seen one in twenty years. And then I remembered that my last tape recorder was replaced by my CD Walkman that I used when I used to remember to exercise, except the CD player was sort of janky and wouldn't play unless it was held flat, so I'd power-walk through my neighborhood holding out the CD player with both hands in front of me like I was in a very big hurry to present a small waffle iron to someone just around the corner. And now I just forgot what I was writing about and had to go back to remember that I was writing about forgetting what I was fighting with Victor about, and now I'm mad at Victor because technically he started all of this.

These arguments with Victor usually end with my yelling, "YOU

KNOW I HAVE A HOLE IN MY HEAD THAT THINGS FALL OUT OF SO JUST BECAUSE I CAN'T TELL YOU WHY YOU'RE WRONG, THAT DOESN'T MEAN YOU'RE NOT WRONG." Victor will say, "You are impossible to argue with," and I agree, but mostly because I'm pretty sure he knows he's wrong too. I wouldn't be mad if he hadn't done something awful to begin with, and it's even worse that I'm not able to remember the fight. Basically I think I should have a golf handicap but in fighting, but Victor says that doesn't exist and then I just give up.

In fact, I suspect I've divorced Victor several times but every time I tried to pack up the car to leave he threw his suitcases in the car and said, "I can't believe you agreed to go to [*insert name of beach I've already forgotten here*]," and I was probably like, "I—wait, what?" and he was all, "Don't pretend you've forgotten again. You agreed to [*insert thing I have pictures of but don't remember*] but we're gonna have a blast!" And then I doubt my sanity again, because why would I pack dishes to go to the beach? And then Victor would be like, "Yeah, you're weird," and I'd shrug, and then we'd go on an unexpected vacation I'd immediately forget instead of getting divorced. Basically the secret to a long-lasting marriage is memory loss and well-meaning lies and beach margaritas.

It's gotten a bit worse as I've gotten older, possibly as a side effect of the drugs I take to manage my anxiety, or just an effect of growing older, or maybe just my brain becoming as lazy as the rest of me. It doesn't often bother me but it is unsettling how people who read my blog or books will sometimes remind me of things I've done but have forgotten. Or they'll ask me to inscribe a quote in their book and I'll say, "Oh, that's so lovely. Who wrote that?" and they'll look at me for a moment to see if I'm joking and then say, "You. You wrote that." And I did. Or another me did. One of us did, and I suppose that's what matters, even when it's unsettling. If it stays like this forever I'll be okay with it, because I usually forget it's an issue and there are pleasant surprises that pop up when I've forgotten I bought something for myself or suddenly find something important that I forgot even existed. But it's still a bit scary.

Dementia runs in my family very strongly. My doctors don't think I have it, yet, but if I live long enough I'll probably get it. My grandmother has it. I remember her joking about getting it when her parents dealt with it. My mother jokes about it now and I do too, because you either laugh or you cry. Mostly we do both. We pray that if it comes for us, it comes in the way it has so far for my grandmother, who is still as bright and happy as ever even if she can't grasp who you are. She reads the same first chapter of a Stephen King novel every week and talks about how much she likes it. Then she forgets she read it and starts over, enjoying it anew each time. It's a bright spot to a horrible and frightening disease, and a reminder that our time is limited and that our minds are fragile and wonderful and unreliable things. Maybe for some of us more than others.

I've seen family lose themselves and felt the sadness as they look at me without recognition, but I've also seen them later remember everything perfectly. It's all there. Just locked away. For safekeeping perhaps. It's a comforting thought that I can already relate to myself. I have a hole in my head where I fall through. It's all in that hole, I suspect. It's real. It's true. It's locked away in a treasure box. Just because I don't remember, it doesn't mean it didn't happen. And if one day I look at you and don't remember who you are or how much you mean to me, know that your importance is still as real then as it is now. Know that you are locked away someplace safe. Know that the me who loved you is still sitting on that beach, forever feeling the sunlight. And know that I'm okay with not having that memory right now, because the me that holds it tight is keeping it safe and uncorrupted and glorious. And she loves you. And I do too.

Remember that.

For me.

Six Times I've Lost My Shoes While Wearing Them: A List that Shouldn't Exist

If you are a normal person you probably looked at that title and thought, *It's not actually possible to lose your shoes while wearing them*, but I have proven this wrong so many times that I have to assume it's a very common problem that everyone is just too afraid to talk about, and I'm going to be the super-brave person to admit that it has happened to me. *So many times.*

I lose things a lot but usually in relatable ways, like when I can't find my glasses because they're on my face, or when I'm looking for my vodka and it's already in my stomach, or that time when I couldn't find my cell phone so I called it with the house phone (which no one, including me, knows the number to and is solely used to call lost cell phones). Unfortunately I'd turned the ringer off, but I could hear my cell phone buzzing near me, although it was really muffled, and I was searching all over my office but it was nowhere, so I hunched down to listen to see if it was in the desk drawer but it sounded like it was coming from even lower than that, so I crawled under my desk and it was louder but there was nothing there but carpet, and I was feeling around and put my ear to the ground like I was Gordie in *Stand by Me* listening for oncoming trains and my cell phone was like, "THE CALL IS COMING FROM INSIDE THE HOUSE. LITERALLY," *because I could feel the vibrations coming up from the floor*. And I'll admit that I am somewhat irresponsible, but it takes a special kind of careless to somehow leave an entire house on top of your phone, and I was both baffled and also a little impressed with myself. I told Victor that my phone was trapped under the house and that probably we were having an active haunting because only a ghost could have done this and she had obviously put my phone under the floorboards to lead me to her corpse, but he insisted that was impossible, so I calmly explained, "I HAVE POKÉMON GO ON THAT PHONE AND I JUST CAUGHT A PERFECT SNORLAX AND I WILL PRY UP THESE FLOOR-BOARDS WITH A CROWBAR IF NECESSARY," and he didn't entirely believe me because I don't think we own a crowbar and also I don't have any upper-body strength, but then I was like, "What if I just start a small, controlled fire . . . ?" and suddenly he was down on the floor with me glaring at me and telling me that there was no way that my phone was under the floorboards because we didn't live in a horror movie, but then he grudgingly put his ear on the floor and was all, "Huh," which is Victor-speak for "Oh my God, once again I am totally wrong, my delicate pumpkin flower."

But then he paused and was like, "You're probably sitting on it. Get up." And I backed away to show him that there was nothing under me and I was like, "Way to blame the victim, dude," but then he pointed out that the floor wasn't buzzing anymore and that's when I realized that the buzzing sound was following me and I was like, "THE CALL IS COMING FROM INSIDE ME," and that sounds sexual but it's not because, turns out that it was in my dress pocket the whole time, which was sort of a relief but also a little disappointing because now we'll never know if there are corpses in the crawl space.

But this is not that story. This is about actually losing shoes while wearing them, which sounds crazy but happens a lot. I think technically it's my foot's fault, because my right foot is slightly bigger than my left, so I'm always wearing a shoe that's slightly too large on my left foot, and to make it worse I have rheumatoid arthritis, which means that my feet sometimes swell up several sizes (like the Grinch's heart if his heart were in my foot), and then my shoes are all stretched out when my feet shrink back to normal, causing what I refer to as "the Drunken Cinderella Effect" or what Victor calls "At-This-Point-I-Think-You're-Doing-This-On-Purpose." And while I do prefer to be barefoot, I do not like to be wearing just one shoe, because then you're lopsided and it feels like you have accidental temporary polio. (No one gives themselves polio on purpose, Victor.)

Still, he can't understand how it keeps happening, so I'm going to explain it here so you'll understand what's going on when you meet me and I'm maybe just wearing one shoe.

ONE

I was walking out of a crowded elevator into the lobby of an intimidating hipster hotel on the way to a book signing, but in the rush to get out of the crowded elevator I accidentally stepped out of my left shoe, and I immediately knew what had happened because the lobby floor was freezing on my now-naked foot, but I couldn't get back in because the elevator had refilled with people and I was too afraid to push my way in and get my shoe, and so I just watched my shoe take a ride in an elevator without me. And I stood in the lobby with one shoe on as people waiting for tables at the fancy bar stared at me while I feverishly hit the elevator button to get the elevator to return, but it was one of those hotels with four elevators and all the wrong elevators kept coming, and other people waiting for the elevator would gesture for me to get in since I was obviously in a hurry (and also probably insane), but I just explained, "Wrong elevator," which was probably confusing for everyone since all the elevators were going up. I considered explaining what had happened but I was afraid I would get arrested for public intoxication and then I'd have to explain that I wasn't even drunk, and that's almost more embarrassing, because losing your shoe while very drunk is pretty understandable but losing it while mostly sober is just careless and mortifying.

And then the right elevator came BUT MY SHOE WASN'T IN IT and I was a bit flabbergasted because *who steals one shoe?* It wasn't even a good shoe. And I only bring one pair of shoes with me on trips because I'm a light packer, so I couldn't go buy another pair, because most shoe stores require you to be wearing shoes when you enter (which is a terrible vicious cycle), so I just stood there in the lobby as I realized how fucked I was and finally I had to go to security with one shoe on and say, "I think I need to file a police report. Your elevator ate my shoe." But then the security guy called on his walkie-talkie for help and another security guy loudly responded, "Hang on. Is it a black size eight and a half with a Dr. Scholl's insert?" And I was like, "YES. THAT IS MY LOST CHILD. And also, you don't have to point out my level of shoe trashiness, asshole." But I didn't say the last part because he was right and I was just happy to know that Thelma (I call all my left shoes Thelmas; the right ones are Louises) was found and wasn't being used to plant footprints and frame me for a murder.

Apparently someone had called security to report the wayward shoe. I guess they'd kept the elevator stopped while they made sure it wasn't a bomb or maybe investigated how some trashy Cinderella had made it as far as the elevator. Then the security guard brought my shoe down to me and I gave him two dollars because I don't know how much you're supposed to tip for your own shoe, and I vowed to never walk out of my shoes in an elevator ever again, and I never did until I totally did it again one week later.

TWO

I walked out of the exact same shoe while exiting the San Antonio airport parking garage elevator, and I got so flustered that I knocked my suitcase over, so I couldn't make it back in before it went back up. Luckily I was wearing a long dress, so I just pulled my foot up like a flamingo so it looked like I only had one leg. And it was fine, except this young couple with *way* too many scarves for Texas lightly sneered at me when I almost fell over (because I'm bad at balancing on one foot). I stared at them pointedly for being the kind of assholes who would judge a one-footed woman and I felt very self-righteous until I reminded myself that I *wasn't* actually one-footed and was just pretending to have lost a leg to hide the fact that my shoe was currently riding an elevator unsupervised. And then when I got my shoe back I ended up standing in security behind the scarfy couple, who looked at each other in confusion as they tried to decide if I had a twin or had simply grown a new leg like a starfish.

THREE

I was at a bookstore and I wanted to ask if they had any of my books that I could sign, but it makes me very nervous to talk to people and that gives me fight-or-flight. (Note: Fight-or-flight syndrome is what a lot of people with anxiety deal with during stress. My choices seem to be to either shank the person who is making me scared or get rid of all my fluids so I can run faster. I choose peeing over stabbing. *You're welcome.*) So I took the elevator to the bathroom, but when I ran out of the elevator I . . . honestly, do I even need to explain what happened at this point? Basically elevators Patty Hearst my shoes, and it's a problem. And *again* the second elevator came and I was like, "NOT YOU. I WANT THE OTHER ONE," and now there were two women standing beside me, and they looked at my one bare foot and I was like, "Go ahead," and pointed at the elevator I'd just called, but they were like, "Oh, you first," and I was like, "Oh, I'm not going up. I'm just waiting for a shoe." And they stared at me and I was like, "Not like a date or anything. It's not Grindr for feet. I just got my shoe stolen by this elevator," and the ladies were like, "You know what? We'll take the stairs." And then another couple walked up and I didn't want to explain again so I just got in the elevator with them and stared stoically at the ceiling and tried to pretend that it was an avant-garde fashion choice to just wear one shoe, but when I got off the elevator I found that the right elevator was now back downstairs and my shoe was basically joyriding. So I hit the button to call the elevator again and finally the right one came, except that when everyone exited my shoe was gone. Again.

So I went to the front desk and said, "This is going to sound weird, but I'm looking for a shoe," and the girl was like, "*This is a bookstore?*" and I explained that I wasn't there to *buy* a shoe, I was looking for the lost-and-found to see if someone had turned in a shoe because their elevator ate mine. She asked, "What does it look like?" and that seemed weird, because exactly how many single shoes stolen by elevators are turned in to their lost-and-found? I pointed at the shoe I was still wearing and said, "It looks like this, except there's not a foot in it." And she stared at me and I added, "Because I'm not wearing it. Not that I leave shoes with human feet in your store. That would be inappropriate." And then another clerk brought me my shoe and that's why I can never go back to that bookstore.

FOUR

Same year. Different shoe. I was walking into the bathroom of a restaurant and I sort of tripped and my left shoe flew off my foot and skidded across the floor under three stalls and hit a woman in the ankle. And the lady in the first stall yelled, "WAS THAT A SNAKE?" which seems weird because I don't know how you'd confuse a shoe with a snake, but then the first two ladies were like, "A SNAKE?" and put their feet up just in case, and the lady in the last stall was like, ". . . Did someone just throw a shoe at me?" If I had been thinking straight I would have said that I threw my shoe at the snake and been lauded as a hero, but instead I panicked and ran out of the bathroom with one shoe on and told Victor that we had to leave immediately because I'd just accidentally kicked someone who was pooping. "Why would you do that?" he asked. I considered explaining the meaning of the word "accidentally" to Victor but I was too freaked out, so instead I said, "I JUST KICKED SOME-ONE WITH THE GHOST OF MY FOOT AND NOW WE HAVE TO LEAVE." Victor refused to go because he'd just ordered, so I hid my bare foot with my purse until the bathroom emptied out, and when I went in my lone shoe was sitting on the sink and looking not nearly as ashamed of itself as it should have been.

FIVE

I was running through the mall parking lot during a thunderstorm and I stepped into an ankle-deep stream of water and one shoe filled with water and flopped off and was whisked into the storm drain and now it lives with the alligators and clowns.

SIX

I was at the movies and went to flush the toilet but recently someone had told me that I should always flush the toilet with my foot because that way you don't have to touch the handle. Frankly, I didn't even have a problem touching the handle until I found out that everyone else was flushing with their foot, because that means you're all scraping the bottom of your gross shoe that you're wearing in a public toilet on the handle. So basically now I have to flush with my foot too because you people are troublemakers. Unfortunately, because I was new at it (and because my movie theater now has a bar), I lost my balance and fell into the wall and that's when my shoe hit the toilet seat *AND FELL INTO THE TOILET*.

Toilet water splashed on my dress.

I wanted to set myself on fire.

I yelled, "SHIT," and the lady in the stall next to me hesitantly asked, "Is everything okay?" and I said (a little too loudly), "EVERYTHING'S FINE. NOTHING IS IN THE TOILET." Which is a weird thing to say in a bathroom because the very reason you go into the stall is to leave stuff in the toilet, but I'm used to leaving pee rather than articles of clothing so I wasn't really my best self. I stood there, balancing on one foot because I didn't want to put my naked foot down in a public bathroom, as I stared at my shoe at the bottom of the toilet and realized this was going to be one of those moments I would remember forever.

I did not pull my shoe out of the toilet because I think that's how you get cholera, but I did leave all my cash (almost $4 and a half-used Starbucks gift card) on the toilet tank as an apology to whoever did. And then I made a new shoe out of paper napkins and some rubber bands I had in my purse, walked out to my car with what little dignity I had left, drove home, put on a new pair of shoes, drove back, and pretended like nothing had happened. When Victor asked why I'd missed so much of the movie I stared at the screen and just said, "Diarrhea," because no one ever questions diarrhea and it was easier than saying, "The toilet ate my shoe because I do all the things wrong."

SEVEN

I don't have a seven yet, but I suspect I will by the end of the week, so I'll just leave this here.

And yes, it's a little mortifying admitting to all of these moments, but the good thing is that whenever I see those lone shoes on the side of the road maybe now I'll say, "Oh, someone else knows my struggle," and I'll feel a little warm inside. And then Victor will say, "Hang on. Is that one of *your* shoes?" which is offensive because not all stray lost shoes are mine. You should be grateful, because now whenever you see a lost shoe on the highway you can think of me instead of worrying that UFOs or serial killers or UFO serial killers are abducting people.* YOU'RE WELCOME, WORLD.

---

* Victor says he's never thought that, but he also says he doesn't think there are dead bodies in those black trash bags on the side of the road, so it's pretty clear that he's a liar and doesn't listen to enough true crime podcasts.

And Then I Bought Condoms
for My Dog

Last week when I was at the pet store they were pushing a giant display of dog shoes. I immediately felt guilty for not realizing this was even a thing my dog needed. Dorothy Barker is a papillon whose feet are the size of Pixy Stix, so I was pretty sure that none of the dog shoes would stay on her feet. The clerk suggested I try these waterproof, disposable rubber dog boots, but I'm pretty sure he was just trying to sell me a sack of outrageously expensive deflated balloons.

I did the math and it came out to like a dollar per paw, which meant I would be paying four dollars just to let my dog wear balloons on her feet. And I thought to myself, *Is this a test? Is this how they see if buying a dog has made you lose your damn mind? Is it like when you buy tiny $100 shoes for newborn babies whose feet never touch the ground? Because I never fell for that shit either.*

So then I was like, *Fuck this, I'm crafty. I'll just make my own damn dog boots.* And I probably would have but Dorothy Barker is tiny, so all of Hailey's water balloons were huge on her feet and she just walked right out of them. So I went to the drugstore and the clerk asked if he could help and I said, "Yeah. I'm looking for tiny condoms. Like *toddler-sized tiny.*" And he was like, "Uh . . . ," and I quickly explained, "I mean, not for me. *Obviously,*" and he laughed in semi-relief and I said, "They're for my dog."

And then he stopped laughing.

"They're not for her penis," I said. "She's a girl dog. She doesn't even have a penis. I need condoms for her hands." And he looked at me weird but probably just because I said my dog has "hands" instead of "paws" and maybe because he thought my dog was into fisting. Which she's not, because I don't even think dogs do that. "*Not for fisting,*" I added.

The clerk looked at me like he wasn't sure if I was fabricating a dog to cover up my demand for tiny condoms, so I clarified. "They don't even need to be penis condoms. What about those finger condoms?" and he said he wasn't familiar with the concept so I was like, "Well, you've obviously never worked in food services," and then he looked even more uncomfortable.

I explained that finger condoms are what you put over your finger if you have a cut so you don't get salt in your wound or blood in the food, and he was like, "*OH!* You mean finger cots!" and I said, "No. Not at all," but then he pulled them out and turns out finger condoms are called finger cots, which doesn't make any sense because I pointed out that a cot is a shitty bed whereas finger condoms are more like tiny waterproof sleeping bags. He didn't respond, and I realized that I didn't even know what size finger condom Dorothy Barker would need and they came in boxes of 1,000, and the last thing I needed was 996 tiny, unusable condoms that were too big for my dog, so I asked if I could bring my dog in to try them on and he said he'd have to check with his manager. I suggested that they sell finger/dog condoms because they could offer them much cheaper than the pet store and he looked baffled, which I get because finger/dog condoms are probably something better marketed on Etsy. Then I decided to stop talking because this was the same drugstore I picked up my drugs from and I thought it was better to perhaps not give them another reason to not fill my mental health meds. (Although possibly this all might make them fill them quicker. Hard to say really.)

Then I went home and told Victor that I was going to make a fortune selling finger condoms to dogs on Etsy, and he said that dogs don't have fingers and that I wasn't allowed to go back to the drugstore again alone. I explained about the waterproof rubber dog boots and Victor was like, "Aren't dogs' feet already waterproof? *Why is there a market for this?*" and then I was like, "Shit. You're totally right," and that's how Victor ruined the only business plan I've ever had.

It's probably for the best though, because I suspect in the Texas heat the condoms would just melt to the sidewalk and I don't want to end up in court after someone's dog gets stuck to the sidewalk because I didn't thoroughly test its condom. Regardless, I'm sort of stuck in research-and-development hell regarding dog condoms, so in the end I decided to just let Dorothy Barker go barefoot—or maybe Scotchgard her.

But it turns out that my concern for Dorothy Barker's feet was misplaced. Because last night she couldn't sleep and tried to go out to pee at least ten times. So today I took her to the vet and the vet was like, "Your dog has a urinary tract infection and canine vaginitis." I knew what the first one was but the second one was new to me, so the vet was like, "Her cooter's all borked up. That'll be three hundred dollars."

Then she said, "I'm giving y'all some medicated wipes. You'll need to clean your dog's vagina four times a day," which seems excessive because frankly I don't even clean *my* vagina that often.

But then I got home and Dottie refused to let me near her lady garden and I was running after her yelling, "LET ME WIPE YOU," but she growled and hid under the table and I was like, "YOUR VAGINA IS A GROUP EFFORT, DOG," and then she tried to bite me and I was like, "LOOK, I'M NOT TRYING TO SHAME YOU. I ASSURE YOU THIS IS ALL PERFECTLY NATURAL FOR A WOMAN," and then Victor came out of his office and yelled about how hard I made it to be professional on conference calls and I was like, *"Don't blame me. Blame your dog's vagina,"* and then he was like, "Welp, see you later."

I finally decided that it might be easier to wipe the dog's hoo-hoo if it didn't have so much fur on it, so I went to Target. They didn't have clippers for dogs, but they did have a ton of trimmers for men's grooming and that seemed close enough. I was overwhelmed by the selection and didn't know which one to choose. The lady stocking the trimmers asked if I needed help. I explained that I was looking for the best way to shave my dog's vagina and she was like, "Oh." I explained that it was for medical reasons, *not recreation,* but she still looked disturbed, and then I realized that maybe she's one of those people who is very pedantic about the term "vagina" meaning the tube part of the lady garden (and honestly it *would* be weird to shave inside a dog's vagina), so I corrected myself and said, "My dog's *vulva*, I mean. *Obviously.* You know what I mean." But it started to seem like she really didn't at all, so I grabbed the cheapest clippers with the ear-hair attachment because it seemed like if it was safe for ears it was probably safe for dog vaginas.

Unfortunately, Dottie didn't understand that I was just trying to help and she got freaked out by the clippers and kept running from me, so I had to wrap a towel around her head so that we didn't have to make eye contact and share our mutual shame (which is probably the same way I'd want to get a bikini wax if I'm being honest). She calmed down a little, but I was holding her like a burrito in one hand and the clippers in another hand and she got squirmy and I accidentally cut a giant hunk of fur off of her tail and now it looks like she tried to cut her own bangs, if her bangs were on her ass.

Then Victor yelled at me for breaking the dog but *she was already broken before I started shaving her, Victor, and I have the doctor bill to prove it.* Technically she seemed pretty happy to have a freshly shaven vagina, and she ran around the house feeling the breeze on her downstairs apartment and showing it off to anyone who would look.

My point here is that I manage to mortify myself enough on my own, so I don't really need a dog helping me out. She's very lucky that she's adorable, because I didn't even want a dog and now I'm spending my days fitting her with condoms and grooming her broken lady garden, and at this point I want a trophy. But just a basic one that says I'm a good person. Not one specifically for excellence in dog genitals.

No one wants that.

Probably.

Rainbow Fire

I have struggled with anxiety for as long as I can remember. When I was young I thought it would pass as I got older, and when I was older I thought it would pass when I was successful, and when I was successful I thought that it was hopeless because even when everything was going right I was still wrong.

I think I was six the first time I got stuck.

I remember hiding in my toy box when I was little, pushing out the toys on the bedroom floor and closing the lid over me to hide from the strangely unnerving and irrational fear I didn't have the words to explain. Sometimes I'd just stay a minute and sometimes I'd stay so long that the dark became colorful blurs that danced in front of my eyes. It was a safe place for me, until I got stuck. Not stuck like you might imagine, like the time my little sister sat on top of the lid to mess with me. That was fine, actually, because it felt weirdly safer—like I had a tiny bouncer doing security. The first time I got stuck, though, it was scarier because the thing trapping me inside the box was me.

I listened to my heart pound in my ears as my mom called for me. It was time for day care, as my mom had to work. I knew that when I crawled out of the toy box I'd have to go to that place that all the other kids seemed to like but that sent me into a vomity crying panic as soon as my mom left my sight. Nothing truly terrible happened at day care. I just panicked at every moment and cried myself sick with worry that I wouldn't see my family again, that I'd get lost, that my sister would run into traffic . . . crazy things that seemed so real to me. My mom called for me again. I knew I'd get in trouble for not coming but I couldn't move. I was paralyzed with dread. I knew it was crazy but I couldn't open that lid.

But my mother could. When she opened it the light hurt my eyes, making me realize how long I'd been hiding. I wasn't ready. Emotionally or physically. My mom carried me to the car and did everything she could to help me, but soon my anxiety wore on her as much as it did on me. She'd be called by the day care dozens of times, because I had cried myself sick, because I'd locked myself in the bathroom, because I refused to take off my coat since if I left it on I could pretend she'd be back any minute. Eventually she quit and got a job at my school as a cafeteria lady so that she would have the same hours I had. She never said it was because of me, but I think we all knew it was. I would have liked to say, "It's okay. I can do this," but the truth was that I couldn't.

The anxiety attacks never really went away. They would get better and worse throughout my life, with no real rhyme or reason. Over the years I'd hide in bathrooms and closets and books. And mostly in myself. It was a lonely place to be, but safe. Except when I got stuck. When the fear of leaving the bathroom would be so severe that I'd miss my next class or meeting because I couldn't make myself leave. When the fear of lifting my eyes out of a book made me pretend that I didn't hear classmates who tried to get my attention and then made fun of me for ignoring them. When I fell so far into my own head that I couldn't see how to get out of it.

This has never entirely gone away. Therapy and medication helped, but still, I had weeks or months where I was stuck.

A few years ago I was on tour, promoting a book I'd written about my struggles with mental health. It was doing really well, which meant large bookstores filled with wonderful people who often dealt with so many of the same issues that I had. So many came and shakily told me that it was the first time they'd left their house in weeks. I recognized those scared eyes and the terrible frayed exhaustion of these kindred people who were ready to run at any moment. I felt proud and happy that I was able to talk to each person but also ashamed because it was so draining that it was all I could do to survive the anxiety of being away from my home, and every spare moment I spent hiding in hotel rooms, recovering from or preparing for the anxiety of being around people.

I was traveling through North America in cities I'd never seen before and I was wasting these opportunities to see the world. I couldn't leave my hotel room. I didn't have the strength to visit the amazing places that were offered to me even when they were just outside my door, and I hated myself for it. I understood, and I empathized with myself, and I told myself (correctly) that if I used the massive amount of energy it would take to go outside I wouldn't have the strength left to visit with people who came to my readings. I know it was the right decision but it didn't stop the feelings of failure and shame over something most people could easily do.

At one stop I was in New York in a hotel that overlooked Times Square and Carnegie Hall and all these places I wanted to see but couldn't. I looked out my window at locations that might as well have been on Mars. I got dressed and decided to go outside, if only for a minute. But I couldn't. I stood at my hotel door, and it might have been a brick wall as I stared at it and shook and cried and felt completely broken. It's not even something you can complain about without feeling stupid. I was being given such an amazing opportunity and I was losing it and there was nothing I could do about it.

I curled up next to the window, opened it, and leaned out, feeling the breeze on my wet face. I told myself that it was like being outside with the rest of the world, even if it wasn't. I watched tourists walk into Carnegie Hall and imagined what it looked like inside. And that's when I saw it.

Down below my window was a fountain, shaped like a dandelion. A giant ball of pipes that dwarfed the people walking by it, and each pipe ended in a fountain, like a firework made of metal and water. I'd seen it before and it was nice, but it was something different now as the wind picked up and carried the mist of the fountain heads upward and it caught the light and created an enormous rainbow wall that waved with the water, like fire made of colors.

It literally took my breath away as the rainbow fire grew higher and became something organic and lifelike, a giant organism coming alive, and I grabbed my phone to capture it before it disappeared. And that's when I saw the second-most shocking thing I'd seen that day.

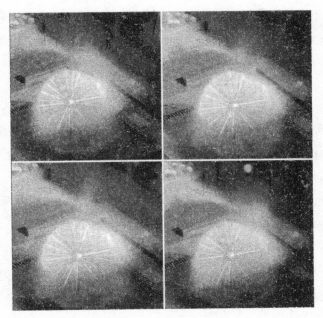

I assure you, if this picture were in color you'd be impressed.

I saw that no one else even noticed what was happening.

Hundreds of people rushed by the fountain. No one stopped. No one looked up in awe. It was one of the most beautiful things I'd ever seen and no one else seemed to care.

At first I thought that it was because they were all just so used to this rare beauty that to them it was old and boring, fading into the background. But then I realized that it was something else entirely.

I was the only one who could see it.

The sunlight had hit the fountain from between the buildings so that the dancing rainbow fire prism was only visible from where I was . . . from the small room I was stuck in. It remains one of the most brilliant and awe-inspiring things I have ever seen in my life. And it occurred to me that I would never have seen it if I hadn't been trapped in my hotel, having a small breakdown . . . if I hadn't been right in that spot right at that second. It was all about perspective, literally and figuratively. I considered it a sign that perhaps there is a path I'm supposed to be on. It's not the same path that everyone else takes, and that can be hard and lonely, but I was reminded that there are amazing things I would never see with normal eyes and other paths.

I cried again, but this time out of a small thankfulness that my brokenness set me in the place where I am. Beautiful, terrible, unseen by most, unique.

I wish I could say that seeing that fountain inspired me to leave my room that very minute so that I could see other amazing things, but it didn't. I wasn't ready and life isn't as easily wrapped up as that. But sometimes it gives you treasures and reminds you that maybe, just maybe, you're in exactly the place you're supposed to be after all.

All of the Reasons Why I'm Not
Coming to Your Party

If you are anything like me, you know that socializing can be truly terrifying (in my case, both for myself and everyone near me). In fact, if I've ever spent any time around you I should probably take this time to apologize for making it weird. And if I didn't that's most likely because you are just as awkward as I am and are blind to it, or because I just wasn't given enough time. Trust me, I am bad at people to the point where I sometimes fantasize about how great house arrest might be.

This is precisely why I have kept this running list of horrific things I've said to strangers and colleagues during uncomfortable silences, which usually led to more uncomfortable silences. I write them down when they happen so that whenever Victor insists I have to go to an office party I can just pull out this document and read from it, and after a few minutes he's like, "Oh, right. I don't know what I was thinking."

NON SEQUITURS I HAVE SAID OUT LOUD THAT DID NOT GET THE REACTION I HOPED FOR

- Did you know that you can get rabies and not even know it because bats have such a tiny bite you can't even feel it and they have an anticoagulant in their spit so they can just lick you all night while you sleep? You're like a never-ending gobstopper for bats. That's why one-night stands with bats are generally a bad idea and also why I sleep in footie pajamas. Sure, it's not sexy, but you know what's even less sexy? Getting your toes sucked like they're a crazy straw by diseased winged rodents with foot fetishes.

- I think being bilingual is underappreciated. "I love you" in German is "*Ich liebe dich*," which is pronounced "ick leeby dick." The nice thing is that you can shout it at your husband when you're fighting and it sounds like you're calling him an icky leaky dick, and then when he yells back you can be like, "I WAS SAYING 'I LOVE YOU,' YOU HURTFUL TURD."

- People say that it's good to be a woman because they can have multiple orgasms, but it seems like anyone can have multiple orgasms if they're patient enough. I can't help but think we're getting credit for something that's not really that much of a benefit. It's not like we're having a race. And if we are, I suspect men are ahead of us anyway.

- People say that blood is thicker than water, but since when does thickness equal importance? Pudding is thicker than blood but I'd still rather have blood. Unless it's for dessert, I guess. Then I'd rather have pudding.

- I just realized that the order of the alphabet is completely random. It's not in alphabetical order because that was invented after the randomness of the alphabet, so how did we decide that this was the order of the alphabet? Are other languages' alphabets in the exact same order? WHO STARTED THIS?

- There are about twice as many human nipples in the world as there are people, but there are about as many human testicles in the world as there are people. Like, it averages out to one testicle per person. That's a weird story problem.

- My friend Bonnie told me that figs have wasps in them and that's why they're crunchy, but she probably just didn't want to share her Fig Newtons.

- Did you know that drone bees die when they are mating with the queen bee because during their orgasm their testicles explode and their genitals stay inside the queen? I can't even decide who it's worse for, the drones who just watched their friend get his nuts popped to death or the queen, who is like, "WHY DOES THIS KEEP HAPPENING?" Anyway, that's my theory for why all the bees are disappearing.

- If I had a nickel for every time I hypocritically felt better about myself for not being one of those other hypocritical people who self-righteously brag about being better than other people who aren't as enlightened as they are, I'd probably have enough money to actually fix some of the things that none of us are really doing anything meaningful about.

- Why do we say "dropping like mayflies"? What is it about May that's so dangerous to flies?

- I sort of feel like the "stir halfway through cooking" microwave dinner instructions are just a trick to make stupid people waste their time so they have less time to bother the rest of us. And I appreciate it.

- I wonder if Neil Armstrong ever gets tired of people constantly asking him about a place he vacationed in for less than a day sixty years ago. The moon is basically a rock with no air and I have to imagine that Mexico is just as interesting.

- Someone gave me a poster that says, "Let her sleep for when she wakes she will move mountains," and I think it's a nice sentiment because it encourages people to not wake me up, but I already can't sleep because tomorrow I have to go to the bank and I can't turn off my brain and now I'm finding out that I HAVE TO MOVE MOUNTAINS? I'm probably only sleeping late because I was up all night worrying about mountain relocation. Maybe the mountains need to stay where they are. Why is this my problem? Fuck this. I just scratched out the part about moving landmasses and left "Let her sleep" standing. Because I don't throw babies out with the bathwater. In fact, I don't throw babies at all. Or move mountains.

- Yesterday I lost my phone and so I called it from the landline so that I could find it, and then a few minutes later I noticed that I'd missed a call from Victor so I called him and he claimed he hadn't called me and I was like, "You are a liar because I have a missed call from you," and then I realized that the call was from me pretending to be someone looking for me and that I was gaslighting myself.

- This morning I was writing about brussel sprouts and spellcheck told me they're actually "brussels sprouts." With an S. Like they're from Brussels? Because I'm in my forties and I just now figured that out. My whole life has been a lie.

- I wonder if the word "um" is universal in every language. If so, why "um"? The word we're stalling for statistically probably doesn't start with an "um." Unless it's "umbrella." We should instead replace "um" with "I" because most sentences start with "I." Which would work because even if you stretch it out and can't remember the word, you can just drop it to "I . . . can't remember the word I'm looking for."

- Victor tried to make me feel bad because I never got Hailey a birth certificate, but in my defense I didn't get one because they're like baby receipts and I'm not gonna get a refund. Then Victor said that they're not for returning babies, they're to prove that you have a baby, but I already have proof that I have a baby and her name is Hailey and she lives here.

- People always say less is more, but it seems like more is more. If less is more, then less is possibly too much. Now my head hurts even more. Or less. Maybe both.

- Yesterday I sent a text to Victor saying, "You are the wind beneath my wings," and then he wrote back, "What?" because turns out I'd accidentally typed, "You are the wind beneath my legs," and then he was all, "Like a fart?" Yeah, Victor. *Like a fart.*

- I was at the grocery store and the clerk said, "I think you have a sticky note on your boob," and she was right, and it just said, "FEED LIZARDS TRASH," and I explained that it was a reminder to feed my daughter's lizards and to take out the trash, and that I didn't just feed trash to random lizards because that would be fucked up. She agreed but I'm not sure about what part.

- Considering all the famous people who've been cremated and dumped into the wind, I've probably breathed some of them in. Which is sort of rock and roll if you look at them like cocaine, but they're not cocaine, they're corpses who shouldn't be inhaled. It's more like a famous person entering your body without your permission, and I think that means I've had unprotected sex with famous people through my nose holes, which are the worst holes to have sex in. Plus, what if it's someone who was really promiscuous? Now I've been with everyone they've been with. Unless you start over again after cremation? But even so, if they're all invading everyone's nose holes, then it's like I not only had nostril intercourse with a famous person, but I also had nostril intercourse with everyone else who breathed them in. Unless they ended up in a Kleenex. I wonder how many ashes just end up in Kleenexes. Probably lots. They should advertise that. Kleenex, I mean. Not cremation. "You'll end up in a nose hole" is a terrible tagline. But maybe: "Kleenex: Now with aloe to cradle the corpses you exorcise from your nose." (Needs work maybe.)
- Are the Wright brothers and Frank Lloyd Wright related? Because that seems like an unfair amount of talent from one family.
- Has anyone ever reimagined *The Giving Tree* but the tree was the stalker instead of the other way around? Because if not, I call dibs.
- Math says the shortest distance between two points is a straight line. Unless the line makes you drive through a lake or a brick building. That shit is gonna slow you down. Math makes a terrible taxi driver.

- I'm not sure what the difference is between sleeping and time travel.

- I was looking for new cups but there was a note on the top shelf of the store that said, "Please do not touch yourself. A staff member is happy to assist you," and I laughed a bit too loud and the clerk totally didn't understand why and I said, "Oh . . . you know . . . masturbation?" There may have been a communication problem because she asked me to leave.

- People say nice guys finish last, but I'm okay with finishing last, because who wants to hang out with the assholes in the front? That sounds miserable. Nice guys finish last but they get to be surrounded with other nice guys, and you know what nice guys bring? Free cheese. Margarita machines. They'll give you a ride home later. They won't even yell at you for being sexist for using "guys" as a universal name for humans because they're nice, and even if you're stupid they're like, "Oh, bless your stupid heart. You can still sit with us." Fuck the people who finish first. Get them finished and off to drowning kittens or whatever it is they do when they're done. We've got margaritas to drink and kittens to save. Bring your own kitten.

- I keep reading in exercise magazines that I should exercise more, but why should I trust these magazines since they have a vested interest in making me buy them? I don't buy them though. I steal them from my shrink's office, because these magazines make you feel bad about yourself and most of us don't need any help with that, so technically I'm saving people from articles like the one I just read about kegeling. Apparently, I'm supposed to be kegeling all the time to "lift my pelvic floor," and that's ridiculous because now I'm supposed to be exercising a part of me that people don't even see? This is an obvious scam. Next they'll be telling you to make your pituitary gland do squats or flex your testicles. Honestly, I'm not even sure why you would want to lift your pelvic floor, because if your pelvis gets higher the only place it could go is up into your stomach, so basically you just shrunk your torso, which makes you look even thicker, and now you start to buy the magazines out of desperation because your tough new vagina accidentally made you look fat. Plus, they really push the kegeling on older women, but most of us are already shrinking as we age, so basically we're turning ourselves into compressed accordions with terribly muscular vaginas. Is there a magazine for that? No. There isn't. *Because no one wants that.* I have a theory that if you don't do kegels your pelvic floor will drop and then your vagina will have high ceilings, which is very classy when you're looking for a condo so I think the same reasoning applies. Sure, you might pee a bit whenever you cough, but maybe your pelvic floor will get so loose that your ovaries will fall out. No more PMS, plus those things probably weigh five pounds each, so you automatically lose weight. I'm not a doctor but this all seems pretty basic. Also, spellcheck keeps underlining "kegels" and saying that it doesn't understand what they are. JOIN THE CLUB, SPELLCHECK.

• Hailey asked if she could be an astronaut when she grows up and Victor was like, "The sky's the limit," and I pointed out that if the sky was the limit then he'd just grounded her from being an astronaut, because space comes after the sky.

Then he said that he couldn't have grounded her if he'd said the sky was the limit because if you ground a plane it means they can't go into the sky, and I was like, "Touché." And I'm not sure we ever clarified to Hailey that it was all semantics, so it's possible my kid thinks she can't be an astronaut because of Victor's poor grammar.

- I'm pretty good at grammar except for the fact that I continually misspell the word "grammar." But in my defense, it rhymes with "hammer," and no one is spelling it "hammar."
- I wonder if crabs think humans walk weird.
- My dog is ten times as fast as me even though she's tiny, and I'm guessing it's because she has twice as many legs as me, so does that mean that centipedes are a billion times faster than dogs? Because I've seen them before and they don't seem fast. Unless I'm only seeing them when they're really tired. Like maybe they're so fast you can't even see them, and that's why you never see fast centipedes, because we only see them when they're totally winded. Maybe that's why they're so creepy. Because deep down we know that they're faster than the speed of light. Maybe the sound of thunder is just the noise of centipedes creating sonic booms. I'd ask a scientist but I'm afraid they'll steal my theory for a grant. We're going halfsies, scientists.
- I asked Victor if he'd rather touch dog poop or human poop and he told me to go back to sleep, but I insisted it's a good question, because you'd probably pick dog poop, since for some reason it seems less gross than human poop, but technically we should be more used to human poop, since you touch it every day if you're lucky, and then Victor was like, "First off, why would you touch human poop every

day and how is touching it lucky? Secondly, GO WASH YOUR HANDS AND NEVER TOUCH ME AGAIN," and I explained that I meant that we touch poop with our buttholes as it leaves our body and if you're lucky you poop every day, and then he said that the act of pooping isn't the same as "touching poop" but I'm pretty sure it is, because no one poops without its touching you. Otherwise that'd be the immaculate conception of poop. He said that your poop touches *you* but *you* don't touch it, but I disagreed and suggested that we compromise and just agree that he and his poop touch each other, and then he said we could *not* agree on that and also that I wasn't allowed to wake him up at two a.m. anymore for feces-related discussions. And I get that, except that we are still debating it, so it's actually a really great question that should be used to match couples in online dating services. Victor says that no one is going to go on a dating website that asks if you touch the poo or if the poo touches you, but technically the question would just be weeding out the people who run away from the question rather than debate it at two a.m., because this is the sort of endurance and creativity you need to stay married for twenty years.

Thus ends my collection of the thirty-three most recent terrible things I've said to strangers in awkward public outings. Victor has a foolish and wildly misguided hope that one day I will run out of awkward, rambling non sequiturs, but I console myself with the knowledge that at least I'll end up with other terrible things to add to this list. That's one of the few things that are wonderful about being a writer. It's all good because even the most terrible moments make interesting material. Material that could probably be used against me in court in some cases. So I guess it's not *all* good, now that I think about it. But sometimes I'll say these ridiculous things and someone else will be like, "I, TOO, AM FASCINATED BY PUBIC WIGS AND REAL-LIFE CANNIBALS," and suddenly you have a new best friend. Plus, the other people at the dinner party have a collective reason to roll their eyes at each other and I'm pretty sure that's how you build community.

Samuel L. Jackson Is Trying to Kill Me

I've been broken for a long time. More broken than usual, I mean. I don't know exactly how long it's been because I can't trust my mind. Six months . . . maybe more. Some of it is my head and some is my body, like they're competing to see which one can murder me first. I wouldn't take bets on that race. Either way I lose.

This is one of the downsides of having a body that wants you dead. All of these little autoimmune diseases build up and avalanche into each other, and suddenly everything in your body is attacking everything else because it thinks it's attacking a foreign body or a weird new plague, but the plague is just me. I can't tell my body to just settle down because it won't listen, so instead I take pills and injections that are toxic and unhealthy but less unhealthy than dying from my own body killing me. It's like shooting yourself in the foot because at least that way your body will be too busy trying to recover from the gunshot to keep destroying all your joints and sucking out all of your blood.

Just try to imagine that. Imagine me looking at the blind soldiers in my body who are literally attacking all my important parts and me yelling, "STOP THAT. I NEED THAT," and they're like, "CAN'T HEAR YOU, MA'AM. TOO BUSY DESTROYING THESE DRAGONS," and I'm like, "THOSE ARE THE JOINTS THAT HOLD MY BODY TOGETHER," and they're like, "*WELL ACTUALLY* THEY'RE DRAGONS. THIS BODY IS FILLED WITH DRAGONS. AND SNAKES. WHO LET THESE MOTHERFUCKING SNAKES IN THIS MOTHERFUCKING BODY?" (because my blind soldiers are mansplainers and also Samuel L. Jackson for some reason), and then I yell, "JESUS CHRIST, CALM YOUR TITS. YOU WANT SOMETHING TO FIGHT ABOUT? *I'LL GIVE YOU SOMETHING TO FIGHT ABOUT*," and then I stab myself in the leg because then my dumbass body soldiers will be like, "HA! BLOOD LOSS DETECTED. WE TOLD YOU THERE WERE SNAKES AND DRAGONS IN HERE," but at least they'll go focus on the knife wound and leave everything else alone for a second.

Except when they don't, which is often, because I have a lot of autoimmune disorders, and so even if one is in check at the moment, the others can go crazy, and some of them cause me to not be able to think straight. Which means I can't write or work or sometimes even do basic things like get up and walk around or read or follow a movie. They often trigger illnesses that typical people would think of as "real" because they show up more visibly. Like in the last month I've had walking pneumonia and a separate gastric attack that was so bad I ended up in the ER. Those things are hard and scary, but they fade, unlike the disorders I'll carry with me until I die or until science cures them, so while outsiders say that they are happy I'm better (because they see that I'm no longer coughing up a lung from the same bug that gave everyone else mild sniffles) they don't see the fog in my head that hasn't lifted or the ache in my bones or the deformities in my joints or the toxins in my blood or the exhaustion that is so intense I find myself lying on the floor because I didn't have enough energy to get to the couch. I watch writing opportunities pass me by. I see deadlines loom and pass and latch themselves to my back like hungry ghosts, and I see my family worry and care but also (as is human) get tired of my being tired. And I get it. I'm tired of it too. They see me ask the same questions over and over again because I don't remember asking them, and they ask if I'm joking sometimes when I start a conversation about something I've already told them about a million times. I'm not joking, but we still laugh because laughter is the best way to cover pain. Not "cover" it as in "hiding it." It's in plain sight. But to cover the black holes of anger or anguish or worry that need to be filled in lest we all fall in instead.

Two weeks ago the latest round of tests found a lot of new problems, but the main ones were these:

1. A lack of testosterone. This is a good one because it causes depression and anxiety and exhaustion and foggy brain, and basically that is what I'm made of, so it could be a miracle cure if it's fixed, but it's been two weeks since I called in my prescription and the pharmacy keeps saying it will be in soon but I'm not strong enough to demand they give it to me. Probably because I don't have enough testosterone. It's identical to when I forget to get my ADD meds filled because I have ADD. This is why I need a drug butler.

2. Pre-diabetes. This seems weird because it seems like "pre-diabetes" means you *don't* have diabetes, so that seems like it should be a good thing, but apparently it's

not. This means I have to go on a low-carb, low-sugar diet for a few months,** and the list of things I can't eat is the same as the list of things that currently keep me alive, so I was like, "What *can* I eat? Ground-up glass? Because that's the only thing missing from this list," and my doctor was like, "Meat. You need more meat. Meat is healthy for you," but I don't think so, because I'm made of meat and I'm inadvertently trying to kill myself all the time, but then she was like, "*Lean* meat," and I just growled because I was already hungry for a mashed potato sandwich and also I thought my doctor had just called me fat. So currently I'm eating meat, greens, and my feelings. I've lost twelve pounds, but based on my past luck it's probably my blind Samuel Jackson warriors "helpfully" ridding my body of whichever important organ they've confused with rabid squirrels.

_____

** I've been on this awful doctor-mandated low-carb, low-sugar diet for a month now; the good thing is that I've lost twelve pounds, and the bad thing is *pretty much everything else involved in eating low carb/low sugar*. It's nice that I've lost twelve pounds, but I still have to lose more, and I sort of wonder if I just feel less awful because there's now slightly less of me to feel awful, and by that reasoning I will probably feel my best after I've been dead for six months.

Also, last time I saw my doctor she was putting another woman on the same diet and I was like, "It's a weird diet. You can have all the bacon and vodka you want, but no carrots," and my doctor was like, "That's . . . not really the diet I put you on," and I was all, "*You specifically said no carrots*," and she was like, "Yeah, I'm not arguing about the carrot part . . . ," and she started talking about heart problems but I stopped listening because basically every time she talks I get a new disease.

Also, helpful hint for people on the same low-carb, low-sugar diet I'm on: Get some of those already-roasted whole chickens at the grocery store, because they're delicious and when you rip one apart with your hands you can pretend you're a giant and that it's the torso of the person who put you on the low-carb diet. Additionally, hummus wrapped in lettuce leaves = somewhat filling and also the saddest burrito ever. I plan on staying on the diet for another month or two, but I don't think I can do longer than that because bread is delicious and with all the vodka I'm drinking I might be getting *too* healthy.

3. *All* of the anemias. Including pernicious anemia, which I'm pretty sure is something invented by Lemony Snicket. And the anemias cause all sorts of issues, including making me severely low on a lot of vitamins you need to live, so my lab work was thirty pages of "Bitch, you are *all* the way fucked up." Basically it means that I'm missing a lot of blood for no reason, which sort of makes sense because I lose shit all the time, but it seems like if I was misplacing blood I'd remember, or at least Victor would yell at me for leaving all my blood around like he does about the dozens of half-filled glasses of water all over the house. "Missing blood" seems a little disconcerting, like when you're missing time, except usually that's because of alien abductions, so at least you have a reasonable explanation.

There can be a lot of reasons why I'm so anemic and exhausted and sick. Some of those reasons are simple, and some are scary, but personally I'm leaning toward attic vampires. It would explain the blood loss and also the rustling I sometimes hear upstairs late at night. Victor says it's squirrels on the roof but *what would squirrels want with all my blood, Victor?* He is the worst detective ever. Also, it would make sense that vampires are after me, because I may have offended them when I refused to pay them off a few months ago.

Short interlude here while I explain that I was recently contacted by "the Vampire Brotherhood," who told me in broken English that I should send them money for immortality. I did recognize it as an email scam, but it was such a creative scam I felt that I could not refuse, so I immediately struck up a conversation with them.

Dear Vampire Lord,

I am not currently a vampire but I like the idea of not dying. I want to be skinnier, though, before it happens. Or do I automatically get skinnier like in Twilight? *Also, I'm a vegan. Is that a problem?*

Hugs.

You are welcome to the family but before we start you have to fill out a form and send a photo of you so I can send it to the High Master. I await the above form before we can start the initiation of you becoming a member of the VAMPIRE BROTHERHOOD.

~Master Paul

Thank you for your quick response! I am still very interested in becoming a vampire but I'm concerned about the name of the association . . . THE VAMPIRE BROTHERHOOD. I am a lady and therefore do not have the requisite penis necessary to be a "brother." Also I'm a feminist so I worry about the connotations of an exclusively all-male vampire society. Even in the afterlife I have to deal with a patriarchal oppression? We're better than that, aren't we? Please let me know if you're okay with my vagina and also if you are open to changing the name of your organization to something a little less nineteenth century. Perhaps something like UP WITH VAMPIRES? Your call.

Hugs.

In this brotherhood we have a female as a member and that name has been there and we can't change it. Keep this all as your own secret and migrate from fear. You are unlikely to be dead. Now we shall proceed on your initiations and you will be a full member.

~Master Paul

"You are unlikely to be dead."

I'm confused. Am I unlikely to be dead because I will soon be a vampire and thus undead? Or are you telling me I'm unlikely to be dead because you won't literally turn me into a real vampire? I've been burned before. (Not literally.)

What I mean is that you will leave as you want on earth because you will be given immortality.

~Master Paul

I will want to leave earth? I live here. I can't be a space vampire. I don't even have a passport. Also, once I'm in, can I turn my dog into a vampire too? Because I'm not going through eternity without Lil Schnitzel. He's hypoallergenic and will make a great vampire. He's a small dog and he lives in my purse because my apartment has a no-dogs policy but I say I don't technically have a dog living in my apartment if his paws never touch the ground. My landlord disagrees but all this will be moot after Lil Schnitzel is changed because who is going to kick out a vampire dog? No one, that's who. This is a deal breaker.

Oh! One more thing. My ex-boyfriend Brad Dingleman CANNOT be made into a vampire. I was telling him about it before I found out he was cheating on me with my best friend and he might try to contact you and join and I DO NOT want to be running into Brad Dingleman for the rest of eternity. Trust me, I am doing you a favor here too. This guy is a real dickhole. Also, he was all, "I'm gonna be a vampire first because I already have a jeweled ascot," and I was like, "I think you're confusing vampires with the rich guy from Gilligan's Island," but he insisted, so can you settle this argument? There isn't a dress code for vampires, right? Except for capes, I'm assuming. I'm fine with capes. I can rock a cape like Liberace. Just, if you have an application for Brad Dingleman, put it in the NOT THIS GUY pile and be glad you dodged a bullet. Metaphorically, I mean, since you are immortal and not affected by bullets.

Unless you trip on them, I guess?

Unless you can fly when you're a vampire and you never fall. OH WAIT. Is that what you meant when you said I could leave the earth? That I'll be all floaty and shit?

Oh my God, I'm so in.

The Vampire Lord responded to that email but the response was blank, which I assumed was the email equivalent of stunned silence, but then he came back with:

If you are ready to join then you must pay the charge amount for the vampire blood, which is 150usd.

~Master Paul

Very relieved to hear from you! I assumed my former association with Brad Dingleman had scared you away but I can assure you that as soon as he removes all those eagle carcasses from my freezer (he's a hunter) I will never see him again. That guy ruins EVERYTHING.

Quick question, is the $150 bag of blood enough to turn me and Lil Schnitzel or do I have to order a separate doggie bag of blood for her? She is a very small dog (three pounds if you don't include her jewelry and tiara) and I am concerned about her overdosing if I give her too much. Although I guess if you overdosed on vampire

blood you'd just be extra immortal? I'm sorry. I'm sure you get these
questions over and over.

Hugs.

I was ignored for twenty-four hours, so I reached out again.

I haven't heard from you in a bit and now I'm worried that
Brad has gotten to you and convinced you that my dog and I
would not make good vampires. That motherfucker cannot be
trusted. You can ask any of the girls who work with me at Apple-
bee's and most of the ones at his gym. Also, I suspect maybe
my pro-feminism stance earlier left a bad taste in your mouth

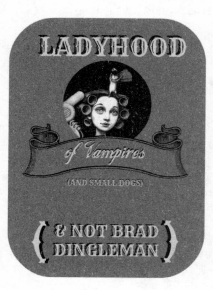

because you were so adamant
about not changing the name
to something less patriarchal,
but personally I just think
this is a good opportunity for
rebranding. See proposed new
logo, attached:

Pretty good, right? This is the
kind of high-level marketing I
can bring to the team. Brad can't
offer this level of sophistication.
He can't even text without using
emojis and last week he sent a pic-

ture of his junk to everyone in his contact list. Including his mother.
Including MY mother. You probably got one too. He is an idiot.

Aaaanyways, Lil Schnitzel and I are starving so send those
blood bags over. Preferably COD because I'm a little concerned
this is a scam and I'd like to see the goods first.

Hugs, the Countess and Lil Schnitzel the Dark One (Just trying it on for size. It sings, right?)

Then I got ghosted by a vampire so I went undercover to see if I could score some blood by posing as a man.

Specifically, Brad Dingleman.

Hey, I'm ready to be a vampire. Hook me up.

—Brad Dingleman

PS. (oYo) = BOOBS. LOL

Coming as a surprise to no one, Master Paul and the patriarchy were all over Brad Dingleman and responded to him within minutes, offering him immortality for $10 less than they were going to charge me and Lil Schnitzel! Needless to say, I did not feel bad at all for catfishing Vampire Paul and I never emailed him again.

And *that's* why you can't trust vampires, and also probably why they're stealing all my blood and why I have all the anemias. Did you forget that's what we were talking about? Because we were, and I totally understand why you forgot, because my head is a mess too. Probably because of attic vampires.

My doctor, however, is firmly in the "It's probably not vampires" camp and thinks it might be a bleeding ulcer but they need to be sure, so next week they're going to drug me up and stick one camera down my nose all the way to my intestines. Then they put another camera up my booty pipe all the way to where the other camera stopped, like some terrible river cruise gone horribly wrong.

Hopefully they're different cameras, or they at least wash them well. I suppose they could be disposable cameras, which would be good because I wouldn't have to worry about having a camera that's

been in a thousand people's buttholes going up my nose, but I suspect either way my blind soldiers will see it and will be like, "AH, WE
**FUCKING TOLD YOU THERE WERE SNAKES IN HERE.
NOW THEY'RE ON VACATION AND CARRYING AROUND
SELFIE STICKS AND TAKING PICTURES LIKE A BUNCH
OF GODDAMN TOURISTS."** And they would be right, in a way,
and I plan on asking the doctor if I can have a copy of the pictures
so I can literally have the *most* introspective #nomakeup #iwokeup-
thisway Instagram photos ever. I also want to ask if they do the scopes
at the same time, because if so I would literally be a shish kebab for
a few seconds, and considering how little I've accomplished in the
last six months it would be nice to at least be able to put that on my
résumé. "Writer, illustrator, humorist, shish kebab."***

Sometimes I can find the humor in all of this, but it doesn't
change the fact that I worry when this happens that it'll never
go away . . . that this is the end. That I'll always be waiting until
tomorrow, when I'll have strength to be funny or to make sense
or to shower. I know I've had periods like this before, so logically
I know that I should be okay eventually. That I'll come out of it.
The problem is that depression is my forever side dish to any
period of convalescence and illness, and depression lies. It tells
you that you are worthless. That life was never good. That you are
a drain on the world and that it will only get worse.

It's probably not true. It's not true. That first line is what I feel.
The second is what I know. But even knowing it, perception feels

---

*** I am a snake swallowing its own tail. And also I'm allergic to snakes. Additionally, the
pill cam data came back and the doctor was like, "You're all fucked up but we still don't
know where all your missing blood is going. Your stomach looks gross, though, and you
have ulcers." Probably from the stress of all these tests. Long story short, my body is trying
to kill me and I want a replacement. Or a cyborg body. I'm not picky.

like reality when you're in it. That's why nightmares are real to you when you're asleep even when they seem so ridiculous when you wake up. You wonder how you could have ever been terrified of enormous puppies with your mom's head on them that chase you into a swamp made of quicksand and fire, but at the moment those terrible mother-puppies were all you knew of reality. And then you wake up more and realize that your mom in your dream was Kathie Lee Gifford and *WTF, brain*? And that's sort of what depression is like . . . like when your mom turns into Kathie Lee Gifford's face on giant, murderous swamp puppies. If you don't have depression this analogy might seem baffling, but if you have it you're probably pointing at this page and saying, "FUCKING BINGO, LADY. YOU NAILED IT." Which is probably what I will say to the doctor during my shish-kebabbing, because apparently I'll be in a twilight state and last time I was in one of those I thought leprechauns were trying to get me, so God knows what I'll say. Maybe I'll live-tweet it.

I try to look on the bright side. If I were still working in HR I'd have to be on disability now, but since I work from home I can adjust my schedule to my broken body and my mind. I can still afford the expensive medications and doctors' bills and there are a lot of people who can't. I'm lucky. I could be sicker. I could be dead.

I could be dead.

I wrote that twice because I'm saying it with two different emotions. One where I'm so grateful to be alive and another sneakier, terrible thought where I realize that if I do die I'll get some rest. That's fucked up. I know it. And as soon as it hits my mind I shoo it away because I know it's the depression, but this is a place for honesty, so there it is.

Last night I sat under the stars with Victor as he tried his best version of a pep talk by reminding me that we have bills to pay and that I owe my publishers a book and that we can't just get by forever with only his salary, but it didn't really work because fear galvanizes him but it paralyzes me, and I ended up a sobbing mess while Victor looked scared and confused and said, "Shit. What did I do wrong? I was just trying to help." And he was. But his talk wasn't really what had scared me. It was what he'd said a few minutes earlier, when I was worried that all of these disorders were catching up with me . . . that maybe the scoping would find something bad . . . that this was the beginning of the bad kind of avalanche. I didn't explain it properly, or even at all, because my head wasn't working and I couldn't find my words in time to insert them in the conversation where they were supposed to go. I consoled myself by musing that if they did find something, at least I have life insurance, so Victor and Hailey would get some small comfort out of it, and Victor looked at me quizzically and said, "*You don't have life insurance*," as if I should have known that, but I didn't and I was shocked, because that seems like the kind of thing that he would take care of. Then he said, "*You know this*. Remember? I have life insurance but you don't. We went through all sorts of hoops to try to get it for you but you insisted on telling them all the stuff that was wrong with you and we couldn't get it approved. Remember?"

I don't. But I believe him. It must have happened. And maybe when my body rights itself all of these missing memories will come back. Or maybe they won't. Either way, it was a blow, and one I'd already suffered through before apparently. Possibly even one I've written about before and have forgotten. I didn't have life insurance because I was "a bad risk." Which seems a bit ridiculous because it's not like Victor is not at risk of dying too. He's totally going to die. We all are. I mean, it's possible that some of you are vampires but for most of us even the healthiest person is at a pretty high risk of not being immortal. I think the only difference between me and Victor is that I'm more likely to die before the guy who is selling the insurance policies and probably most everyone else will die after that guy is already dead, so it won't be reality to him. It's like global warming for elderly people. They probably think it's likely but they know they won't live to see us invaded by polar bears and volcanoes (I don't know how global warming works) so they keep committing arson with aerosol bottles or whatever dangerous things elderly people do for fun (I don't know how elderly people work). Basically, *I'm* global warming. But faster. And with fewer polar bears. (I don't know how good analogies work.)

If anything, life insurance companies should offer me a great deal, because if I die early then everyone I know will see my life insurance being used by my family because I'll make them wear shirts to the funeral that say "Jenny Lawson died and all I got was this lousy shirt. Oh, and also a car and a college fund because life insurance exists and they aren't fuckers," and everyone at the funeral would be like, "Whoa, that life insurance stuff is the shit. Let's buy some!" And then everyone wins. And that would be a nice change because lately it feels like it's been a lot more losses than wins.

But I'll keep going. And I'll keep fighting. And I'll keep forgiving myself for being flawed and human, and if I can't write a funny chapter I'll write a chapter like this. One that might be a little pathetic, might not make sense to anyone but me, but is still true. Exactly like me.

Before we walked back inside Victor hugged me and calmed me and made me laugh.

"I am a bad risk," I said, sighing with acceptance.

He was silent for a minute.

"You are a bad risk," he agreed, nodding as he looked up at the stars. "But one I'm happy to take."

And as I breathed in the night air I thought of the struggle and the glory and the sadness and celebration and mystery that still lay ahead of me.

And I said, "Me too."

And it was the truth.

How *Do* Dogs Know They Have Penises?

Yesterday I was watching my papillon, Dorothy Barker, as she peed, and it occurred to me that boy dogs lift a leg to relieve themselves and girl dogs squat, but how do they know which one to do? I sent a text to five different people asking simply, "How do dogs know they have penises?" Three of them (understandably) ignored me. One said, "Oh I haven't heard this one. How DO dogs know they have penises?" like it was a joke I didn't have a punch line for instead of an important question. The fifth person was my sister and she gave me back hope for humanity.

Me: How do dogs know they have penises?
Lisa: Holy shit. Yeah, how do they know they have penises? They don't have hands and you'd think that looking at their junk would block their view because of where their eyes are. Now my brain hurts.

Me: RIGHT? Like, how do male dogs know to lift a leg and female dogs know to squat?

Lisa: AND WHY WOULD THEY DO THAT? Wouldn't it make more sense for them all to squat? Lifting the leg throws off their balance. Maybe it's just a "cool guy" thing just because they can? Maybe they're trying to show off their penises to other dogs, like mini flashers? NO ONE WANTS TO SEE YOUR DOG PENIS.

Me: Our last dog used to lift a leg and he was so clumsy he'd always fall over onto his back halfway through and pee on himself like a furry little drunk. Squatting would have made so much more sense. I bet if male dogs had thumbs they'd send us dick pics all the time.

My phone tried to correct that to "duck pics."

But honestly the phone is probably right. They'd probably send us duck pics too. Dogs fucking love ducks.

Lisa: I don't think they'd send the dick pics to be rude though. Just to be like, "Have you seen this? It's the darnedest thing. Here. Let me lift my leg and show you." Dogs: the first flashers.

Me: Yeah, there's no aggression there. They might not even know it's a penis. Just like, "Hey, have you seen this? Weird, right? Let's chase squirrels!"

Lisa: Bumble pees on his front legs half the time and falls over randomly. Did you know that bearcat pee smells like hot buttered popcorn and they pee on their feet on purpose? The guy that does the Wow in the World podcast says it's because they are trying to spread their scent around but I bet they just really like popcorn.

Me: What's a bearcat and why am I now jealous of their pee?

Lisa: I think we should request an episode about how do dogs know that they have penises. Go listen and start with "Hot Buttered Popcorn . . . PEE?!?" Then listen to "Stick It Right Here, Sluggo!" because knowing you you'll cut yourself soon and your body will be allergic to stitches, but they discovered that slug slime makes an excellent medical adhesive. Probably not yard slugs. Maybe though. You should try it. For science.

Me: Not worth the smell. Were you there when I accidentally smashed a snail in my pocket at Granny's and it smelled so bad I threw up in the bushes and I had to wash my dress out in her sink and then the indigo dye in the dress bled all over me and I looked like I'd murdered a Smurf?

Lisa: It sounds vaguely familiar. For some people that would be on their highlight reel of memories. In my brain it's just another "that one time that Jenny did something stupid." That's a pretty good snail defense though. You didn't do it again.

Me: I just Googled "bearcat hot buttered pee" and now I have to delete my internet history.

Lisa: Oh, like that's the worst thing you've Googled this week. I always thought the Ballinger Bearcat mascot was a mythical creature but apparently not. They should douse the mascot's feet in melted butter and stuff it with popcorn to respectfully portray the bearcat. Plus, the kid inside would have a snack.

Me: Now I want buttered popcorn. And a pet bearcat. It would be like having live potpourri that also eats all the bugs in your house. I could stop paying the pest control guy. Basically we'd make money on this deal.

Lisa: Except your cats would pee on top of the bearcat pee and they would mix together and you'd have hot buttered cat pee everywhere.

Me: Sounds unappealing. Wikipedia says the bearcat is "curious and very intelligent but highly irritable." It's like if Victor was an animal.

Lisa: Like you need another one of those. It would just complain about the noise.

Me: Victor or the bearcat?

Lisa: Yes.

Me: Victor says I can't have a bearcat because, "No, stop asking. And also they're endangered." THAT IS SUCH A BEAR-CAT THING TO SAY.

Lisa: Maybe the bearcat and Victor could commiserate. Get him one for Christmas. I don't know how big they are (the mascot was person sized but I bet that wasn't accurate since I was a hawk mascot in high school and I've never seen a hawk taller than me) but if it's cat sized you can put it in his stocking. If it's from Santa there's no take-backs.

Me: And obviously they're endangered, Victor. EVERYONE WANTS ONE. They're all hidden inside nicer-smelling houses than ours. This is why we can't have nice things. Because Victor hates bearcats.

Lisa: How does he even know so much about bearcats?!

Me: Maybe he used to be a bearcat and a witch cursed him to be a human. Like a reverse Beauty and the Beast. I've gotta smell his pee.

Lisa: Tell him Jeff Goldblum has several bearcats.

Me: Does he?

Lisa: I mean, probably? I just figured it'd make Victor jealous so then he'd want one.

Me: Update: Victor says he doesn't care how many bearcats Jeff Goldblum has and also he won't let me smell his pee.

Lisa: Well, clearly he's hiding something. You'd think you'd notice if he had great-smelling pee after twenty years.

Me: I should really pay more attention.

Lisa: Now we have to figure out how to break the curse. What do bearcats eat? Offer him that and then we'll know for sure. If it's crushed snails, that would explain why he was attracted to you. You're probably still carrying that smell around with you.

Me: Jeff Goldblum. Dog penis awareness. Hot buttered pee. Curse breaking. We are so full of truths today.

Lisa: If only more people would ask us more things the world would be . . . well, it would probably just be more confusing.

Me: Okay, you said that bearcats eat bugs. I've never seen Victor eat a spider but maybe I've just never plated one properly. That man doesn't eat anything without a plate. Like, not even over the sink. THE SINK IS JUST A BIG PLATE, VICTOR.

Lisa: If you eat over the part with the garbage disposal you're just being extra, extra tidy. They say cleanliness is next to godliness so eating over the sink is basically a religious experience.

Me: Victor hates Jesus and bearcats and happiness.

Lisa: Nothing new there.

Me: Ooh! But that might be a great name for my next book.

Lisa: I doubt you'll do very well with the Christian audience but stranger things have happened.

Me: I've already offended the uptight Christians. The cool Christians are still fine with me. I mean, they're praying for me, but they're also entertained.

I just asked Victor if he wanted to go to that place that serves escargot and he said yes. Escargots are just pretentious snails that went to college, right? Honestly, it's like his inner bearcat is begging me for help.

Lisa: So, 100% without a doubt he's a bearcat.

Me: How do I break the curse? Do I have to make a bearcat fall in love with him even though he's an angry human? *Fuck that.* I'm not letting some bearcat hussy seduce my husband with her delicious urine.

Lisa: Apparently bearcats aren't very social (explains the endangered part) so he probably just doesn't want you to get another one because it would be awkward.

Me: OR MAYBE HE DOESN'T WANT TO CHANCE FALLING IN LOVE WITH A BEARCAT AND BREAKING THE CURSE BECAUSE HE LOVES ME.

Lisa: That's it. It's really quite romantic when you think about it.

Me: Aw, Victor. That is such a bearcat thing to do.

Lisa: So in kindness don't get a bearcat, but do fill his stocking with snails.

Me: I should surprise him with a big plate full of spiders. Because then he'll know that I know his secret and that I appreciate his sacrifice. A big plate of Appreciation Spiders. That is so Modern Romance. Or maybe Postmodern Romance.

Lisa: PoMoRo. I think you just invented a new genre in every bookstore. You can't not say it. Just reading it makes me happy. Like a sassy read. My shoulders get into it too.

Me: And it makes sense because modern art is slightly baffling but then you look at postmodern art and you're like, "Wait, what the shit is happening here?" AND THAT'S TOTALLY ME AND VICTOR.

Lisa: Oh my God, you're right. You ARE PoMoRo.

Me: At first glance it looks like porno. PoMoRoPorno. That's a hard tongue twister for you.

Lisa: That's a Hard Tongue Twister is the name of the first PoMoRoPorno.

Me: They probably won't have a section for that in Barnes and Noble though.

Lisa: "And now, a reading of PoMoRoPorno."

Me: One day statues will be made. Ones that children can't see, obviously.

Lisa: Small statues. But size isn't everything.

Me: Not in PoMoRoPorno.

Lisa: And just like postmodern art it'll be very confusing but you'll get it in the end. (Also, You'll Get It in the End is the name of the statue.)

Me: Victor says we're going to get protestors. They'll chant "NO, NO, NO! NO MO' POMOROPORNO!"

Lisa: That's a mouthful! (Also, the name of the second book.)

Me: All the high fives.

Lisa: Amen.

These Truisms Leave Out
a Lot of the Truth

Recently (when my mind was being more of an asshole than usual) a friend sent me a book filled with small phrases and truisms that are supposed to be inspirational. And they were. In that I read them all and promptly added the parts that the authors had left out.

Those idioms are always a bit messed up. Like, people tell you to "take the bull by the horns," but why? It's a bull. Where are you taking it? And if you are going to take it somewhere I'm pretty sure you don't drag it by the horns. The first rule of bulls is *avoid the horns*. They aren't bicycle handlebars. They're made for disemboweling. Anyone telling you to take a bull by the horns is probably trying to have you murdered in a very lazy way and thinks you are an idiot. Might as well make it "Take the bull by the horns. Then grab the cobra by the fangs. Take Charles Manson by the scrotum. Still alive? Fine. Take poison by the gallon. Take a bunch of rabid dogs and a toaster in the bathtub with you. *Seriously, how are you still reading this? Is this Rasputin?*"

Still, I think it's a good thing to really analyze and fix these truisms, because life is not simple or easily changed by small inspirational words. It is complicated. And hard. And sometimes ridiculous. Much like the truisms I ended up with. So I scrawled my own endings into the book and when I was done I passed it to another friend going through a bad stint of bullshit and she was like, "This is the most helpful book ever," and I started to apologize for drawing in it but then she was like, "No, that's the part that made me feel better. No one wants to hear 'Put on a happy face' when they're miserable, but I was nodding violently in agreement when you added 'Make it the face of that guy who cheated on you with your best friend. Take his face and wear it around a little. Maybe wear it when you peek in your former best friend's window at two a.m. Just a suggestion.'"

It was nice to think that I wasn't the only one who needed a bit more, so I decided to share a few here with you. The truisms are in bold. The rest is my addition. I probably don't need to clarify that.

BELIEVE IN YOUR DREAMS . . . Unless it's that dream where you are stuck in quicksand and your third-grade teacher is a monster chasing you with the times tables you still don't know. Fuck that dream.

ONLY DO WHAT YOUR HEART TELLS YOU . . . Except really it's your brain that is telling you what you think your heart is saying. Your heart can't think. So basically your brain is pretending to be your heart to manipulate you. So maybe do what your heart tells you but make sure your brain knows that you know that it's Cyrano de Bergeracing shit.

LIFE IS LIKE RIDING A BICYCLE . . . It's hard and sweaty and surprisingly tough on your genitals. Also, you're going to fall a lot.

FRIENDS ARE EVERYWHERE . . . So are ants. Watch where you're standing.

IT'S NOT WHERE YOU TAKE THINGS FROM—IT'S WHERE YOU TAKE THEM TO . . . But try telling that to the security guard at the grocery store when you shoplift a bunch of tuna fish to give to the stray cats that live behind the dumpsters at the mall. (I am like the Robin Hood of cats. With more misdemeanors probably.)

IF YOUR SHIP DOESN'T COME IN, SWIM OUT TO MEET IT . . . Except, if it's *your* ship, why is it out at sea without you? Did you not tie it up properly? Are you sure it's even your ship? Because if it's not, that's piracy and it is frowned upon. I mean, you can barely even steal fish for cats without going to jail.

LIVE AS IF IT'S THE LAST DAY OF YOUR LIFE . . . Except don't, because that sounds awful. I'd spend all day in tears if someone said I was going to die at midnight. That's like having to have fun at gunpoint. Maybe start slower. Like live as if it's Saturday even when it's Wednesday afternoon.

BE OPTIMISTIC: SEE THE GLASS AS HALF-FULL . . . Unless it's half-full of poison or cat urine. Although technically it would be better to have a glass half-full of cat urine rather than totally full. Unless it's half-full because you drank half of it because you didn't know what it was. I think the point here is that we need smaller glasses and you shouldn't drink things you haven't poured yourself.

THE BEST THING TO HOLD ON TO IN LIFE IS EACH OTHER . . . Or the remote. Or the phone. I'm always losing those. But I almost never lose people, because I can just call them and be like, "Where are you? Also, have you seen the remote?" Unless I lose my phone. Then I have to scream until someone comes and calls me with their phone so I can find my phone. So I guess holding on to each other is good too in case you need your phone.

DO WHAT YOU LOVE EVEN IF IT MEANS YOU'RE BROKE . . . Exceptions: gambling, heroin, prostitutes, alcohol, and most other fun things.

AIM HIGH . . . Because your blow dart will lose altitude over the distance to your enemies and you need to account for that. Also wind direction.

YOU CAN FLY . . . But only metaphorically. You can't actually fly. I don't care how much PCP you've had. Get off the roof, idiot.

THE WORLD IS YOUR OYSTER . . . It's tough to get into and it will cut you if you don't use the right knife. Also, it's slimier than expected but sometimes you get jewelry. Unless this truism means that you are the pearl and the world is the oyster that you live in? Which would kind of make sense because pearls are technically just natural irritants and that's a pretty good description of human beings in the world.

MY CANDLE BURNS AT BOTH ENDS . . . And that's how fires start. Also, you're dripping wax everywhere. This isn't even how candles work. What are you doing?

IT'S ALWAYS TOO SOON TO QUIT . . . Unless we're talking about smoking. Or spending all your money on lottery tickets. Or being a serial killer. Actually, skip this truism. I need more information.

DON'T LOOK BACK . . . Unless you're changing lanes. Then it's really important to look back. Maybe this should be changed to "Don't be the asshole who just changes lanes without checking behind you." Also, use your blinker.

APRIL SHOWERS BRING MAY FLOWERS . . . And also flash flooding. And mosquitoes. And malaria. But you'll have flowers, so that's something, I guess.

IF THE WIND WILL NOT SERVE, TAKE TO THE OARS . . . Nothing like a good oar to get your kite in the air.

BUILD A SHIP BEFORE YOU BURN A BRIDGE . . . Or better yet, build a ship out of the bridge. Otherwise you're just wasting lumber. Then charge everyone who needs to get across the now-bridgeless body of water. TA-DA! Now you own a ferry service.

IN EVERY MAN A CHILD IS HIDDEN . . . Maybe not every man. Just the one that ate a child. Stay away from that man. He seems dangerous.

YOU CAN MOVE MOUNTAINS . . . But honestly, why would you want to? Seems like you can find a better use of your time. Learn how to knit or something. The mountains are fine where they are, Kevin. I don't want to have to buy new maps.

FOLLOW YOUR HEART . . . But just metaphorically, because your heart is where you are, so technically you could just sit on your ass all day and be following your heart. Although it's nice to keep in mind, because when your husband is like, "HAVE YOU BEEN WATCHING CAT VIDEOS ALL DAY?" you can say, "No. I've been following my heart. Literally. Asshole."

An Open Letter to My Health Insurance Company

Sometimes I think you want me dead.

But the truth isn't so absolute. You just don't care for me to live.

And why should you? It was a mistake to think that an insurance company claiming to want to help you in your sickest hours was anything other than a scam . . . after all, you are here to make money. And I am here to live. And it seems those things are sometimes mutually exclusive.

The first time I thought you wanted me dead was decades ago. My antidepressants weren't covered. This was just after when my husband had to cut off my Internet access when he found me trolling through suicide message boards but just before I got approval for a medication that wouldn't make me suicidal . . . the one you had declined to cover. The one I appealed because there was obviously some mistake and you sent me a letter saying, "We have decided not to cover this medication because we believe it is not medically necessary," and I thought it was a cruel joke, but when I called, you said it was a mistake and you apologized so profusely I felt bad for you. And you helped me with the next appeal and said it would go through and it did. And I was so grateful that you helped me get a medication that I needed that I only had to jump through way too many hoops for.

I don't remember all of the other times when you let me down. They blend into each other. That's the bad part about having a mind and body that fall apart sometimes . . . there are so many opportunities for you to deny. To deny that I need medication. To deny that I sent in the appeals and the paperwork until I prove it again and again. To deny to my doctor that you even existed, constantly sending bills back to me saying I'm not covered even though I've never missed a payment in my life. Making me deal with debt collectors while you said on the phone that you didn't know why it kept coming back as "not covered" and blaming the doctors for inputting it wrong but never helping to fix it.

It's gotten worse but that isn't surprising. Abusive, dysfunctional relationships usually do. I wasted years with you, racked with pain from rheumatoid arthritis. I did what you said, took the medication that you approved and avoided the ones you said weren't necessary. It wasn't until I moved and found a new doctor that she said that I didn't have to be in such pain . . . that there was no excuse to not use new medications that could put me in remission. I cried when she said that because it seemed so wrong. But it wasn't. And now, years later, I'm in remission. On a drug that you do not fully cover. On a drug that you refused to cover at all sometimes. Like when you said you'd only cover it if I would also take an additional medication that makes me horribly sick. My doctor said to just get the extra medication and throw it out. Sometimes lying is necessary. This is what I've learned from you. I watch the bottles of medication I don't need pile up as I wonder if there's another girl who can't get this wasted medication because you won't cover it. That would be crazy, right? Almost as crazy as not covering the antidepressants I've taken for years.

When you first said that I didn't need the antidepressants I thought there was a misunderstanding, because you were fine with them before. It was only when I switched to the generic version and had a breakdown that there was an issue. Apparently the release mechanism wasn't the same in the generic and for some of us that causes a problem. Luckily my shrink quickly recognized the issue and switched me back to the brand name. But suddenly you decided that it "wasn't medically necessary" that I have the drug that had kept me away from suicide. I appealed and appealed and my doctor sent letters and forms and exceptions and you gave excuses for not covering it that were all proven wrong and eventually you relented. It was worth the hours and hours of work, I thought, until I picked up my medication and found it was hundreds of dollars a month.

"But you told me it was covered," I said to you.

"Oh, it is," you explained. "But you have to pay a penalty fine for not taking the generic." A penalty that was even more expensive than the medication itself. And I paid it. Because at least then it went toward my deductible. Until six months later when you decided even the penalty wasn't enough and that the antidepressants I was paying thousands of dollars a year for would no longer go toward my deductible. I cried then. I felt helpless in a system where nothing was secure.

The appeals started again and I felt like a burden to my family and to my psychiatrist, who again (*again!*) filled out forms and exceptions and letters, and you routed her calls to dead ends so often that her assistant won't even deal with you anymore. They don't even accept you there, did you know? You aren't welcome. I pay for my visits myself with cash. And I pay for my antidepressants myself as well. When the pharmacist rings it up they always hesitate, then say, "This can't be right. It's ringing up at almost two hundred fifty dollars." It's right, I assure them. But "right" isn't really the word I'm looking for. "It's what I've come to expect." And they understand, which is even sadder.

Once, when I complained about your rejections ("We've decided not to cover compounded medications anymore"), you told me that I should get on a better plan more suited to my needs. Then you looked me up. I already am on your most expensive premium plan. You'd sent me a pen to thank me. I use it to write thousands of dollars of checks to pay for the things you ignore.

But it isn't really "ignore," is it? Because you know exactly what you're doing. You know my history. You know every moment of my private medical past. You receive documents from my doctors outlining a plan of action to keep me alive and you decide that they're wrong.

I'm not the only one you've done this to. You've left thousands of people alone and desperate and untreated. You have killed people we love, with neglect or indifference. You deny mercy and pain and humanity. I'm not even one of the worst cases. My problems with you are typical. And that makes it even worse.

In some ways I am lucky. At the moment I can afford to escape the life you try to place me in. I still go to the doctors you won't cover. I still buy the medications that I need. Not all of them, though. You've succeeded in making me give up on some, but I still can afford the basics, even though the price is anything but basic. It's upsetting and worrisome, because one day I won't be able to pay your giant premiums and the thousands of dollars out of pocket for the simple treatments I need to live.

It's disappointing and infuriating, but that's not the worst part. The worst part is how cunningly your words echo the terrible lies my mental illness tells me.

"You don't really need that medication."

"It's all in your head."

"It's too expensive."

"It won't work."

"It's a waste of money."

Those lies are difficult to fight when you're dealing with depression. It's even more difficult when your insurance company seems to speak the same words.

One of the hardest things to do when you have depression is admit that you need help and seek treatment. We are exhausted and hate ourselves and don't want to spend time and money on ourselves, but we push through. We do the hard work. Then we are told that the only doctor you will pay for can't see us for two months . . . or the doctor who gives hope with a plan of action is overruled by you, someone who has never met me, who has never seen my pain, who will not mourn the person who will be lost to this. You tell me that I'm not worth the treatment that is already so hard to find. You say it to so many of us. And sadly, some believe it. Many of them can't speak about it now because they no longer have the voice to. So I will speak for them.

Last month things got worse. My fears grew. I worried about what would happen to me when I could no longer pay for my shrink visits and medications. I worried about the side effects that my antidepressants were having on me. I looked into a procedure that my doctor recommended that might help. Most patients have a positive response and more than 30 percent of patients go into remission from depression. It's painful and takes months of work but it's noninvasive and there are no side effects, though it's expensive. My doctor and the doctors at the psychiatric unit that does the procedure agreed I was a great candidate. It did not surprise me that you disagreed. That you blocked the procedure and the appeals. You said that I just needed more medication . . . that I needed to be on the strongest dose possible of a medication that already causes insomnia and sexual dysfunction and fatigue and a host of other side effects. A MEDICATION YOU DON'T EVEN COVER. And that if it didn't work I should try another medication on the strongest dose possible. Perhaps one of the five I've already taken. You wouldn't pay for a treatment with no side effects. Not even a little. The doctors were surprised.

I wish I could say I was.

You say you have my best interest at heart. You are not even a good liar. I'm embarrassed for us both.

I wonder what would happen if I tried the same reasoning on you. "I've received your insurance premium invoice but my conclusion is that this fee is not financially appropriate for you. It is my decision that you should be paid in bags of rocks deposited directly on your testicles. You may appeal this decision by screaming and hitting your head against a brick wall until you get tired. Then read this letter again because I'm not fucking listening." Maybe I'll try that. I don't know.

What I do know is that you are not helping. You are a hindrance—a barrier to treatment—and worse, you are part of the problem. If I were to kill myself today I would first blame my broken brain. And second, I would blame you. You are killing me. You are shaming me. You are standing in the way of the health and happiness of so many of us and you are making money while standing on our backs and telling us how much we don't need the things that keep us alive.

But I am still alive. In spite of you. And I will use this breath to keep living and to remind myself that I am worthy of happiness and health and life and that you are a terrible liar. And I will stoke the anger you breed in me and use it to speak out to others so that they know that you cannot be trusted. Because someone has to look out for the sick people in the world.

And you certainly aren't doing it.

I'm Not Going Outside Anymore.

Today I saw this bug/worm/maggot thing on my sidewalk and it looked freaky and horrifying, and I didn't know if it was highly poisonous and should be killed or highly beneficial and should be brought into the house and bred. I was squatting on the ground staring at it when my neighbor suddenly popped up and said, "Cock chafer?"

And I was like, *This is* exactly *why I don't do small talk*. But I didn't say that out loud because I thought maybe if I just stayed low and kept my head down he would go away. But apparently I was confusing neighbors with hippopotamuses, because instead of going away he said, "*COCK CHAFER?*" *again* but this time more loudly, as if I just hadn't heard him the first time, because apparently he was expecting me to jump at the suggestion. I realized not only that he was not going to go away but that also if he was trying to proposition me he was *really* bad at it, because first, I don't have a penis to chafe, nor would I want to chafe his or anyone else's. Frankly I don't know why anyone would want *anything* purposely chafed—much

less their kibbles and bits—but I didn't have time to respond properly before he crouched down next to the bug/worm/thing and said,
"Yep. That's a real cock chafer."

I wondered if maybe "That's a real cock chafer" was slang for
"That's a real head-scratcher" or "Why are you communing with a
maggot in your driveway?" and frankly it was a fair question because
it really did look like a giant maggot (with tiny feet), and the first thing
I thought about (because I listen to too many true crime podcasts)
was that maybe this was one of those maggots that only hatches in
dead bodies and that perhaps I should look around the lawn for a
corpse, because maybe an unidentified worm and/or an inappropriate neighbor requesting cock chafing was the least of my problems.

It crossed my mind that if this was a death maggot my neighbor
was going to think I was some sort of a serial killer. And that's when I
realized that I needed to say something, because the awkward silence
had gone a few beats too long. But that made me panic even more,

 because how are you supposed
to respond to a bug that is imply-
ing you are a murderer while a
neighbor you've never spoken
to before asks you about chafed
cocks? I'd like to think that the
awkward silence was a sign
that I am a normal person who
doesn't know what death maggots or chafed cocks are, but I
was worried that he might think
the silence was an admission of
guilt (that I was collecting dead
bodies or had been identified as

a cock chafer). But he just cleared his throat a few times, so I looked up and said, "He seems to be doing crunches."

Because he was.

I have it on video if you don't believe me. The worm/bug was flipped on its back and was doing these small abdominal crunches like he was 1980s Jane Fonda. The only thing missing was the why-is-it-so-high-cut leotard. Except the worm/bug didn't have any back legs, so it wouldn't have stayed on, and so probably he'd just wear a tiny leg warmer instead. All of this was happening in my head as my neighbor loomed over me with a look that said, "I have made a terrible mistake walking over here and do not know how to extricate myself from it." And I totally understood, but also I was a little mad, because he was the one who'd started this whole thing by yelling about cocks at me.

Once again I found myself regretting not sending the form letter I'd drafted to everyone on our block when we moved in explaining that I was very happy to meet them and they could come over if there was a gas leak or fire they needed to escape from, but other than that I liked to just pretend I was invisible, because 1) social anxiety, and 2) I'm pretty sure that only psychopaths talk to their neighbors. Victor wouldn't let me leave the form letters on the doors of all our neighbors because he said it was more of a psychopath thing to send out form letters to strangers telling them to pretend I was invisible, but I explained that psychopaths actually wouldn't care at all if anyone talked to them, and if anything I was proving how *non*-psychopathic I was. We'd agreed to disagree on that one, but now I couldn't help thinking that if this neighbor had gotten the letter we wouldn't have been stuck here in this conversation neither of us could escape. I made a note in my head to never listen to Victor again because he is always wrong.

"I mean . . . looks like it, doesn't it?" my neighbor asked, and I briefly thought he was reading my mind but then I realized that he was responding to my witty observation that I was watching a worm do half-hearted sit-ups. "A real cock chafer."

And then I just gave up and asked, "Is that slang? Because I've gotta say, that is a new one for me," and he stared at me in surprise for a second and said, "Um . . . no? The larva you're looking at. It's called a cock chafer." And I must have looked at him in disbelief because he stammered a bit and said, "Humbug. Billy witch. Snartle-gog?" He stared at me. "Spangbeetle?" And I was like, *"Did you just cast a spell on me?"*

He explained that those are the various names this creature is called. "They crawl on their back and eat roots and leaves. I think you call it something different in the South. A doodlebug?" And that's when I realized this guy was nuts, because doodlebugs are those gray bugs that roll up into a dry little ball like armadillos the size of a cupcake sprinkle, and this thing was white and juicy and the size of my middle toe and had a horrible, bitey-looking red head and I was pretty sure Satan had made it, but when I explained that, he said I was talking about a "pill bug," and then I decided we would never be friends, because I'm fine with people calling doodlebugs "roly-polys" but people who call them "pill bugs" or "wood louses" (wood lice?) are generally psychopaths. (Victor disagrees, but again, he's untrustworthy regarding psychopaths.)

Regardless, I found myself in the second phase of awkward conversation, where it turns from awkward silence into a stream of words I can't put back in my mouth. "Why would they call it a cock chafer if it rolls over and moves by doing crunches on its back? If anything it's totally doing the opposite of cock chafing. I mean, regular bugs who drag their undercarriage over the ground are probably always chafing their nuggets, but this guy is intentionally crawling upside down to keep his downstairs business off the sidewalk," I said, and the neighbor stared at me like I was crazy so I was like, "Unless his penis is on his back? Is that what you're saying? Does this bug have a back penis? Or are you saying that the whole thing is a penis because it's penis shaped? Because I don't think that's how science works. Although I've been surprised before. *OH MY GOD, IS THIS BUG ALL PENIS?*"

He stared at me for a second and then shrugged. "That's just its name. I don't think it has anything to do with penises," he said, and then I felt stupid for bringing penises into the conversation and he did that thing where he faked hearing his phone ring and walked away very quickly and I was relieved that the conversation was over, and also I was pretty sure I'd just guaranteed I'd never have to speak to him again.

Then Victor came outside because he'd heard talking and asked, "What are you staring at?" I was still squatting over the worm/bug and I explained, "Apparently it's a cock cruncher," and Victor looked horrified and was like, "*WHAT THE SHIT?*" and I realized I'd misremembered the name so I was like, "No, wait. A cock . . . knocker? Junk . . . puncher? Shit. I can't remember. Something that sounds *very* abrasive to penises. The neighbor just came over and told me and we just had a super-awkward encounter, all because you wouldn't let me send them letters telling them not to talk to me." And he was like, "Start again. Make more sense," but I couldn't because I was *exhausted*.

Instead I looked up "white six-legged worm with red head" and Wikipedia told me that it was probably a European "cockchafer" so my neighbor was totally right. I briefly thought that maybe it was pronounced differently since it's all one word but I went to the online Cambridge Dictionary, which had both the UK and US pronunciations, and the US one was a deep-voiced dude saying "COCKCHAFER" rather ominously and the UK one was a very posh British lady saying exactly the same thing, but somehow classier. It was sort of fantastic and I continued to press the pronunciation buttons so that it sounded like an angry couple in a terrible but very repetitive insult war until Victor came out of his office and shout-whispered that he was trying to remain professional on a conference call and it was very difficult *because why did it sound like an angry international mob screaming "COCKCHAFER" in our house?* And I started to explain that it was just two people but turns out he didn't even want an explanation and that's when I realized that this little cockchafer had ruined Victor's afternoon. And then I sort of thought that maybe that's where the name came from.

Probably not, but it feels right.

PS: I used the word "genitals" too much in this chapter so I went on Twitter to ask what a gender-neutral word for junk was and I got three hundred responses in ten minutes without a single person's questioning why I was asking. A few of my favorites that I didn't get to share earlier: "niblets," "nethers," "naughty bits," "no-no zone," "squish mittens," "Area 51," "the danger zone," "the south 40," "the situation" (with a suggested circular hand motion near said area), "the Department of the Interior," "crotchal region," "fandanglies," "groinulars," "groinacopia," "my hoopty," "my bidness," "my chamber of secrets," "my charcuterie," "front butt," "privy parts," "private parts," "pirate parts" (which I suspect was a typo but now I'm embracing it), and my personal favorite, "the good china." This is exactly why I love the Internet. That and the fact that it's where those fancy dictionary robots that yell "cockchafer" at each other live. *The Internet is a goddamn wonderland, y'all.*

The Things We Do to Quiet
the Monsters

I am not suicidal.

This is what I say out loud. It is what I believe. It is what I *want* to believe.

I am at risk of suicide.

This is what I know. It is what is written deep in my doctor's notes. It's the unsaid thing that lurks in my house.

It's easy to say that suicide caused by mental illness is selfish. And it is. But not in the way that you think. It's not the person being selfish by taking the easy way out. It's the disease itself that is selfish. It steals away the very essence of you and leaves terrible lies in its place. It takes the logic that is true and twists it so that you can't see things that are rational and real. That depression lies to you. You recognize these lies when you are sane or stable or balanced, but when you are in the depths of a depression they seem real. When I'm in that hole I remind myself that my brain is lying and that I'll realize that fully when I recover. And I do. I come out the other side and I wonder how I ever doubted that I'm needed. That I'm worthwhile even if I'm broken. And I write notes to myself reminding future me that right now, *right this second*, I am good and happy and can celebrate and that the lies that I thought were true yesterday didn't win. I write this because I know that soon I'll be low and those thoughts will push their way in and the fight will begin again.

It's hard to live with a brain that wants to kill you. It's not my fault. It's not my family's fault. It's not even real to the outside world. Except that it is. Invisible things can be real. And they're the most insidious because they often convince you that they aren't. So I fight against an invisible monster that lives inside of me. And I am winning, so far. The stigma of mental illness is shifting, I have support, I have medication and treatments and a community and privileges that so many others don't have. *I am lucky*. And with luck and work I will survive the thing most likely to destroy me:

Myself.

At the beginning of this year I was in that dark place. It's a place I visit a lot, but usually not for more than a few days before I come back out. Sometimes it's longer. This time it had been months. Instead of living past the dark days until the sun came back out, I stayed in a depression. A few rare days each month I'd come out and feel like I could finally breathe again. And then I'd plunge back into the uncomfortable numbness of depression.

I'd go to sleep not knowing if I'd wake up depressed or "normal," and when I did feel normal I was so damn jealous of the rest of the world . . . people who could be around others without feeling exhausted or who could concentrate enough to finish basic projects or didn't spend thousands of dollars a year on medication that sometimes worked and sometimes didn't. People who didn't deal with intrusive thoughts and anxiety and suicidal ideation. People who didn't struggle in vain to stop their minds at night and restart them again in the morning.

In the last year I'd done all the things. I did extensive blood work and took thirty-two pills a day to fix all the vitamin deficiencies and anemias and treatable disorders. I ate low carb and cut out gluten. I went nine months without alcohol. I lost fifty pounds and started walking and swimming. But it wasn't enough.

Years ago my shrink told me that I'd be a good candidate for repetitive transcranial magnetic stimulation (TMS). Even the name sounded terrifying so I ignored her like any sane person would. Years passed and she kept encouraging me to check it out. Here's how she explained it to me (although I'm totally going to screw it up because my brain doesn't work properly when I'm depressed, so don't yell at me):

Certain parts of your brain sort of stop working properly when you're depressed. They go dark. You can actually see it on MRIs. A different part of your brain goes nuts and works crazy over-time when you have anxiety. And the anxiety-ridden part of your brain can hijack the rest of your brain that already isn't working, and that's how you get people like me . . . people with treatment-resistant depression.

TMS sends electromagnetic pulses through your skull into specific parts of your brain and stimulates the part that isn't working, like physical therapy for your brain tissue. There's also a way to use it on the overactive anxiety part that could possibly slow it down to normal.

It sounded like magic, if magic cost thousands of dollars and consisted of wearing a magnet on your head that feels like a wood-pecker is drilling into your skull for forty minutes a day for six to eight weeks. That's not really how magic works, but more than half of the people with treatment-resistant depression see improvement, and about a third go into full remission.

I couldn't even imagine what full remission would feel like but I figured if I was willing to have an invisible bird drill into my brain for months it was a pretty good indication that I needed help. I spent a month researching it and doing consults and paperwork and interviews to make sure I was a good candidate. Finally a local psychiatric unit accepted me as a patient. And I was ready.

(Slightly ranty side note: Getting my insurance to help me, however, took another month of fighting, and it was the biggest hindrance to getting treatment. It makes no sense. You can't fight severe mental illness without mental health programs. Without therapy, medication, and outreach. We rely on these to keep us going—to save us from ourselves. Our families rely on them to help us and to protect the world from us. But actually getting help has been [and continues to be] the most difficult, unrewarding, shame-inducing, and unending project I have ever undertaken in my entire life.

It's hard. You give up. You give up fighting for treatment. Sometimes you give up your treatment altogether. Sometimes you give up on living.

I worked with doctors and the TMS people and submitted appeal after appeal. I fought with my insurance company. I finally submitted a letter to them. It's the one from two chapters back. And then it was approved. I'm not sure why. Maybe they just gave up on fighting me. If I could have cried I would have, but I was too numb. I still had to pay a lot of it, but it helped.

And I'm lucky. I have support and insurance and a voice and money to buy the medication and treatment that isn't provided to me. What about those who don't have those things? We fail them. We fail ourselves. They are our children and our coworkers and our parents and the homeless person on the street and the boy who will marry your child and the girl who will save your life. They are the insurance clerks I speak with who tell me they deal with the same problems. They are us.

If you've dealt with this bullshit and you're still around, I salute you. It is hard and embarrassing and makes me furious. You deserve better. We all do. End rant.)

I kept a diary during the treatment because my doctors said it can be really helpful to see changes that might seem too gradual to notice on their own. They were right.

Day 1

I settled into the TMS chair, which looks like a dentist chair but with a computer and a sort of moveable half helmet attached. The doctor told me that before we started he needed to find out "where my thumb lives" and I was like, "Are you sure you're a real doctor? Because my thumb lives on my hand and this all seems like basic doctor 101 stuff," but turns out they have to find it from my brain, which seems like a really long trip, but whatever.

He explained that in order to find the parts of the brain where they need to hit me with magnets, they have to find "the homunculus" first and then work backward, and I thought it was a trick because I've played *Dungeons & Dragons* and I am perfectly aware that a homunculus is a flying telepathic monster made of blood magic:

I pulled it up on my phone to show him and the doctor was like, "Jesus, no. That's horrifying. It's this:"

Worst sex toy ever.

And frankly that's *way* more horrifying than the telepathic winged blood monster, but apparently different parts of your body are connected to specific parts of your brain and they use those connections to map out your brain. To find the right spot they first make you hold your thumb up like a hitchhiker and they keep magnet-punching your noggin until your thumb falls. I called it a "Reverse Fonzie" but the med students didn't laugh because I guess they're too cool for Fonzie.

We quickly discovered that my brain is not at all symmetrical, which I thought was weird, but then the doctor explained, "Well, your face isn't symmetrical so why would your brain be symmetrical?" and that makes sense but it's also a little insulting because basically I think he just said that I'm even ugly on the inside. I responded with, "Oh, like my boobs," because one of my boobs is slightly bigger than the other, and he was like, "I'm sorry?" and in hindsight I think he probably was asking me to repeat myself rather than apologizing but I just smiled because I thought it was really nice that he was so sympathetic about cosmetic boob issues.

Once they found the right spot they started the treatment. It's hard to explain how a magnet that isn't physically moving can feel like it's punching you. It feels like an invisible chisel drilling holes into your head while you have an ice-cream headache and also *you're paying for it to happen to you*. And your head is in a vise and you have tape on your face and your eyes are blinking involuntarily in small convulsions and it looks like you're violently winking at the doctor, the nurse, and the medical students who are all staring at you, and then you explain that you are *not* trying to seduce them but you say it *way* too loud because you have earplugs in to protect your ears from the noise of the drilling and they just smile encouragingly because they're probably used to crazy people saying inappropriate things. I left with a headache that lasted ten hours and a sneaking suspicion this was all an elaborate YouTube prank.

Day 4

It really hurt the first day but the nurse assured me that I'd quickly get used to being pummeled in the skull—which feels like a pretty good metaphor for 2018 in general—and they were totally right. Either my skull thickened or I got used to it, because after a few days I could almost forget I was doing it. I nearly fell asleep once, which I thought would have been ideal because I'd get in a nap, but apparently your brain does different things while you're asleep so you have to be awake for it to work.

They built up the power and intensity, and soon I was doing twenty minutes a day with one magnetic pulse per second on my right side (for anxiety) and twenty minutes with LOTS of pulses for

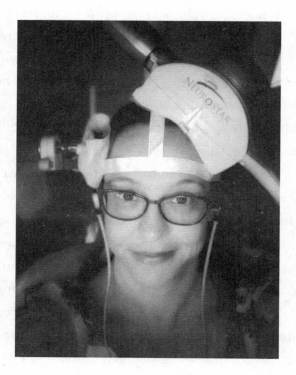

Here is a picture of me in the middle of treatment.

five-second bursts followed by ten-second breaks on my left side (for depression). It's a little like trepanation but not really at all.

They literally put your head in a vise to do this, which sounds like a form of torture. But if you have a good imagination it almost looks like a fancy fascinator for a futuristic royal space wedding. It's basically the most expensive hat I've ever worn. I suspect if I keep doing it long enough I'll develop a Magneto-like superpower, which would be nice to help find my keys or change the channel without a remote.

Day 7

On my seventh day of TMS I felt crazy. And that makes sense because they don't magnet-punch mentally sound people in the head every day (with weekends off). But what I mean is that I felt crazy because I felt maybe this could be working. I went from a full depression at the beginning of last week to a quick (for me) bounce back into "okay" and this weekend I actually felt *good*. Like, I wanted to leave the house voluntarily. I almost went to a museum. That sounds like a small thing but I assure you that it is not.

For the first time in months I felt like listening to music. I avoid music when I'm depressed. It makes me feel too much when I'm raw and it makes me realize how numb I am when I'm unable to feel anything. Instead I fill every quiet second with podcasts . . . anything to drown out the thoughts in my head and pass the minutes until my brain is right again. Wanting to listen to music was a sign I didn't even know I was looking for.

Day 14

I left my session and felt strange but I couldn't put a finger on it. I sat in the parking lot of the psych center and cried. You might think this is a bad sign but it's not. Crying doesn't come naturally when I'm depressed. Depression for me is a painful lack of emotions . . . a disconnection from the world. So in my car when I cried I felt such relief. Then I cried for myself, for the me who'd almost forgotten what it was like to feel human. I recorded myself crying in my car, unmade-up and messy and ugly, because I needed a reminder that this was working. That mental illness was real and that I was worth working for a cure, even if it's temporary.

I had a few dark days but I felt about 50 percent less depressed than when I started. I didn't have insomnia for a week, which was pretty incredible because insomnia is my full-time abusive boyfriend. I noticed little changes, like the fact that I was less likely to tweet terrible things at three a.m. and that I could finally watch funny things. My depression makes me not want to watch comedy because the cognitive dissonance of not laughing at things normal people would enjoy makes me feel like I'm failing at being human, so instead I watch documentaries and horror films because they match my mood. This week I started watching Monty Python again. I laughed and it sounded unnatural. But good.

I'm not 100 percent. I still feel exhausted. I still feel brain fog and anxiety, and the flashes of light in the dark are still flashes rather than steady streams. It might be all in my head, but that's where I keep all my crazy, so that makes sense. It might be a placebo effect, but since I've failed at so many treatments it seems unlikely. It might be coincidence that this bit of sweet relief started not long after the treatment started, and maybe it would have happened normally. I won't know for a while, and even if it works it might not work forever, but I am so clinging to this feeling and to the reminder that things can be good again. The reminder of how sweet it is to breathe again without having to remind yourself that this will pass.

Day 20

Every day I have happiness drilled into my head. The treatments still hurt a little, the magnets drilling and tapping so loudly even over the earplugs. My blinking tic beats out an involuntary pattern with the rhythm and my eyes water. Afterward my skull feels misshapen, my face stiff as I make strange faces on the long drive home. But each day I feel stronger. Instead of feeling like my mental illness is being beaten into submission each session, it feels different. I feel the pulses shooting goodness into my head. *It's worth the pain*, I think. The slow tapping on the right side of my brain, where my anxiety lives, whispers with each pulse: **YOU. WILL. BE. STRONGER.**

The furiously fast drilling on the left side of my brain, where my depression lives: *YouWillBeOkayYouWillBeOkayYouWillBeOkay* *breathe* *remember to breathe*.

I feel different.

On Sunday I think I looked almost like a normal person. I was still scared. With each step I knew I could fall back, that the exhaustion and fatigue and anxiety could hit me at any second. My daughter knew too . . . and she was amazed at each step I took. *Yes, we can go get lunch. Yes, I'll take you to get new shorts. Yes, we can go to the mall, the candy shop, the bookstore. Yes, we can swim and listen to show tunes and sing. Yes, we can play a game. Yes, I'll read to you.*

Yes . . . I'm enjoying this too.

It was the most I've done in a single day in . . . longer than I can remember. And instead of ending the day feeling wrung out and empty and raw, I felt . . . normal? Is this what normal looks like? Because if it is, I want this.

Usually I struggle with simple things. I make strange choices. The strength it takes to shower *or* the energy it takes to eat? You don't get both, so choose wisely. Every action takes such work . . . as if living with mental illness is like waking to a different disability each day. Someone else could quickly do the simple tasks of the day, but I am hobbled. It can take hours for me to do what could be done on a good day in minutes. But not today. Today I feel strong.

I feel guilty for being able to leave the house without Xanax to dull the world . . . for being able to accomplish the things that normal people do every day. And I feel angry that this comes so easily. I shouldn't. I should feel lucky and blessed, but then I remind myself that it's not just happiness coming back . . . it's all of the emotions. It feels like cheating, like I'm on some illegal drug or gaming the system . . . stealing these emotions I forgot were so strong. And maybe that's for the best, because it means that I appreciate how much mental illness takes from me when it is present and how much it's worth fighting for relief. Even with it hiding I know it is a terrible monster I will always fear.

When this monster shows its face I fear the world. I fear myself. I loathe the terrible things that I see and I am too paralyzed to even discuss the news items that stick in my head. My doctor tells me it's not safe for me to dwell on these things and it's true . . . my intrusive, compulsive thoughts make me obsess about terrible things that happen in the world. She reminds me that it will suck away my life if I allow myself to be paralyzed with fear and dread.

I am not built for rebellion. Not yet. My doctors remind me to look for the good in the world, because it is real even if it doesn't get the same press. This is a very good idea for people with broken brains, but mine keeps repeating, "It's not enough. We're all going to die. The world is awful and I am a part of it."

But now, today, it's saying something different. It says that the world is a terrible place . . . *sometimes*. And filled with terrible people . . . *who can change*. But suddenly I'm reminded that there are more people I know who care, who are empathetic, who fight for others in quiet and loud ways. I see that I am not alone. I see how terrible it would be to feel the terror of the world by myself . . . and how heartening it is that I can see so many people doing small and beautiful things to make the world better. I'm reminded (for the first time it feels like) of how alone I would feel if I were the only one who felt disconsolate or frustrated. I'm reminded of how lucky I am to be surrounded by people around the world who care about others. Who are here for each other. I think I knew all this before. But mental illness changes "knowing" and "believing" into two very different things, and I can breathe for a moment and know that it will be okay.

It's an epiphany that brings me such relief. It's going to be okay. Not perfect, never perfect . . . but we will be okay even when we're not okay. Even when we want to be better than we are. It's okay to take a breath. To love and celebrate and smile and mourn and dance and cry and start all over again.

After a Sunday of driving and shopping and dealing with real live people in the loud world, I come home and I am so surprised to find that I am not exhausted. My daughter tells my husband how much we did. "Mom did so great!" she says. As if I am the child. And it makes my heart swell and break at the same time. But I will take this. I don't want to lose it. It feels so shaky. Like holding on to magic you know can't be real.

My husband mentions traveling this summer . . . the beginning of the same argument we have had for years. I can't travel. It's too taxing. I would get sick. I would end up in the same wheelchair I've ended too many trips in. I would slow them down. They go off together on adventures and I am sad but relieved. I've missed many trips. I missed the first time my daughter saw Japan. I watched them on FaceTime from my self-imposed house arrest as they explored the world.

But I will not miss the first time she sees Europe. Because it will be the first time I see Europe too.

I think it surprises Victor how quickly I say, "Okay. You know what? I'll go." He and Hailey hold their breath as if I'll take it back. I hold my breath too. I wait for my body to say, "No, this was a trick. It's not real. You don't deserve this." But it's not saying that. Not yet at least. It's saying, "I want to go. I want to live. I've been waiting so long." It says, "Let's see Scotland and London and Paris. Let's walk on distant islands and explore mountains and see the things that I can't quite imagine really exist because I never thought it would be possible to see them." *But maybe*, a little voice inside my head whispers, *maybe it's possible.*

Maybe.

Maybe this is real. Maybe it's not forever, but it's for today, and if it's real today then there's a chance that any day in the future could be like this one . . . full of promise and energy and an ease I feel like I've stolen . . . one that I feel jealous of even as I experience it.

Next month I will have completed thirty-five days of TMS treatment for anxiety and depression. And to celebrate (knock on wood) I will see things I never thought possible. Some of them in distant lands, yes, but many of them lovely, simple things that the rest of the world takes for granted. I will take my daughter. I will say to her, "Look. Here is the world. It's been waiting for you."

I will say it to myself too.

Please, God, let me still believe it.

Day 27

"What happens if I never get better?"

I have asked Victor this question so many times in the decades that we've been together. There isn't a good answer but he tries.

"What happens if you get better . . . and don't need me anymore?"

This is a question I never thought I'd hear from him. Both because I never thought I'd feel cured or fixed and because it's so ludicrous that I'd only be with him because I'm too broken to go it alone. In fact, I laughed when he said it because I thought it was a joke.

It wasn't. And for once it was my time to reassure him that it would all be okay . . . that nothing could change how I feel about him and that I'm far too lazy to start over with creating private jokes that no one else gets.

I mentioned this conversation with my doctor and he told me this is actually an issue he sees sometimes. One person has become so used to being dependent and the other so used to being a caregiver that when the roles switch it can cause real problems. Dysfunctional relationships can grow worse rather than better. He gave me tools to help the transition and again I was terrified of all the parts of me I'd forgotten since I went away. Victor and I are strong and we can recognize the problems as they come. We've fought demons before. We'll fight them again. My doctor nodded. "I think you'll be fine no matter what," he said. "You don't let your pain go to waste."

It's the strangest compliment I've ever been given. I hold it to my chest on dark days. I wear it as a shield when the fear creeps in . . . the fear of getting worse and the fear of getting better. I think this is what hope feels like.

Day 31

People do different things to distract themselves during treatment. The guy getting TMS down the hall is teaching himself guitar. The girl who has my seat before me draws. I embroider.

It feels fitting. I'm being magnetically stabbed in the head thousands of times as I'm stabbing the embroidery myself. I don't embroider the same patterns my grandmother did. I embroider girls with octopus faces, David Bowie, a flowery bouquet with "FUCK YES" written in the middle. They let you do anything as long as it's "positive." My latest project was a cat, but when you open up the cat's belly there's another cat inside, and Victor was impressed with my stitching but thought a cat dissection was sort of a fucked-up subject, but I explained that it's not a dissection, it's just a cat who wants a belly scratch and then you look inside the cat (*metaphorically, Victor*) and guess what? Surprise! THERE'S ANOTHER CAT IN THERE. CATS STUFFED WITH CATS = TWICE AS CUTE. (Unless it's cats having sex, which is also *technically* cats stuffed with other cats but is less adorable and not necessarily something that should be embroidered on a pillow. Maybe. Depends on the pattern, I guess.)

So, long story short, I think this treatment is making me more optimistic, because if this cat is a Rorschach test I'm pretty sure I'm failing it in the best possible way.

Day 33

Only three more days of treatment left until I'm completely cured! Kidding.

About being cured, I mean. There's no permanent cure for mental illness yet but I have hopes because this shit seems like it's sort of working. I still have dark days and fatigue and brain fog and all that jazz, but I also have bright days . . . lots of them. More than I've had in longer than I can remember. And I have enough energy to go to treatment every single day, and at this point that is sort of amazing.

Last week my doctor told me that when you finally get into

remission from depression you are 350 percent more likely to stay in remission if you exercise thirty minutes a day six times a week. Spellcheck tried to correct "exercise" to "excessive" and *I agree, spellcheck*, but I'm trying it anyway. I'm also sleeping better (which is the first response from TMS for most patients), and that helps with feeling better, and that means I have more energy to exercise, and suddenly I'm almost a healthy person if you don't look at all the bacon and vodka I'm consuming.

Overall it's good, and I'm relieved and scared that it will stop working, but there's another issue I didn't count on, and that's guilt. A little is guilt for not doing it sooner (although if I had done it when it was first recommended they wouldn't have used the more recently approved treatment involving both sides of my brain, so it worked out well that I waited), but mainly it's guilt over using my time for such self-indulgent things. Rationally I know I shouldn't feel this way but it doesn't change the fact that I feel like I'm being selfish. It adds up . . . the hour I spend driving to TMS, the hour I spend in the chair having magnets punch me, the half hour I walk or swim, the hours I sleep instead of work or worry. It feels like cheating. That's wrong. *I know it's wrong.* But knowing and feeling are different things. I know that time given to yourself to make yourself healthier is good for you and for everyone around you. I know that it takes time and effort for some of us to stay sane. I know that I'm worth the work and that I should feel grateful that I can take care of myself without feeling guilty. So the next step is moving from *knowing* to *feeling*.

I don't think I'm alone in this. I think many of us struggle with the thought that it's okay to take care of ourselves, and it's strange that it's a struggle to treat ourselves as kindly as we treat the dog. The dog needs walks and healthy choices and water and play and sleep and naps and bacon and more naps. And love. I need that too. And so do you. It's not just a gift we give to ourselves . . . it's a duty.

I'll remind you if you remind me.

Day 36

Today is my last day of treatment.

Overall, this has been uncomfortable, weird, expensive, time-consuming, and an unnecessary reminder that insurance companies are from the devil.

It was also *totally* worth it.

I am not one of the lucky third of people who go into full remission with TMS. I'm also not one of the unlucky third for whom the treatment didn't work. I'm in that middle ground . . . better, but not perfect.

But better is so good. I've tracked my moods every day these last few months and (other than a short dip halfway through treatment) I've steadily gotten better. I even had five seemingly random days over the last month where I felt what I imagine most people think of as normal. I haven't had days like that in so long I'd literally forgotten I could feel that way.

Every single person is different, but here were my results:

Depression: When I started treatment I was in a deep and very long-lasting depression that I'd been battling for well over a year. I didn't even realize how bad it was until I started coming out of it. I think I was operating at 10 to 25 percent when I started treatment. I'd say I'm between 60 and 75 percent now. I still have depression. I'm still medicated. But this treatment was like a soft reset . . . like turning your phone off and on again when it gets laggy and broken.

Concentration: This is still a struggle for me but I have seen a little improvement. Not much, but a little.

Sleep: My sleep patterns changed the very first week. I still struggle to fall asleep and stay asleep but most nights I'm asleep around midnight rather than angrily tweeting about insomnia at four a.m. I'm less likely to feel like I've been drugged and hit by a truck in the morning.

Anxiety: TMS treats depression on the left side of your brain, but I also did treatment on the right side of my brain for anxiety. This is where I felt the most improvement. When I started TMS I was having severe anxiety and massive problems with agoraphobia. I had a hard time leaving the house and I didn't answer my phone. I struggled with even emailing people. Right now I feel almost normal. Tomorrow I'm leaving to see Europe for the first time in my life and I would never have imagined I'd agree to go on this trip if you'd asked me a few months ago. And I'm scared about traveling but I'm excited, and that's something that I haven't felt in a long time. My family actually noticed these changes in me before I did.

Obsessive-Compulsive Disorder (OCD) and Impulse-Control Disorder (ICD): Unfortunately TMS didn't really improve this a ton. I still feel irrational OCD and ICD thoughts but slightly less.

I don't know if this will keep working, but if I fall into the deep depression again I qualify to get follow-up treatments in the future, and it's nice to have hope. In fact, hope is the best thing that came from this. The treatment is still new and strange and we don't know exactly why it works for some or why it doesn't for others, but the fact that it does work for some people means that there's hope for all of us. Things are getting better and slowly we're figuring out how these wonderful and terrible engines that run us work. I have hope that I will get better. Because I did. And that's a good reminder to keep close when things get bad again and my depression starts telling me lies.

I will get better. So will you. Each day more and more people understand the struggle and more treatments become available. One day there will be a cure. We're getting closer every day. And I'll be here for it.

One Month Later

It's been a month since my last treatment and I'm still feeling good. Not perfect, but so much better than I felt before the treatment started. Overall I think it gave me a few glorious days of true remission but mostly it just pulled me out of the truly terrible depressive period I was stuck in for the last year. I still have clinical depression and anxiety disorder but it feels a billion times more manageable than it did.

I was hopeful that I'd be able to go off my antidepressants, but I don't think that's a safe choice for me so I'm staying on them, although I might decrease the dose a bit if I still feel okay in a few months. I think I could lower the dose right now but I worry about the depression coming back, and at this point I'm terrified to do anything that might put me back in that hole again.

My anxiety is much better than it was before treatment. My agoraphobia is almost nonexistent. I've been slowly cutting down on my Xanax dose and as of this week I officially don't have to take it daily . . . only as needed during anxiety attacks. I hesitate to share this here because I think it's easy for people who don't have anxiety to say, "Good job on getting rid of those drugs!" because most peo-ple don't understand that Xanax (while it has a lot of shit side effects) is a goddamn life raft for anxiety. And while I'm proud of the work I did going off it (because it was hard, honestly), I know that it's entirely possible that I will have to go back on it, and if I do I want to remind myself that that is not a fault or something to be ashamed of. I'm happy and grateful that the treatment I'm on is working better than many of the things I've tried in the past, but what I've learned is that *I didn't fail in responding to past treatments . . . those treatments failed to work for me*. And that is a big difference. One we all need to keep in mind.

Because I feel better, I'm able to do a lot of things to help myself stay better. These were things that felt impossible a few months ago but now seem almost as easy as the people who don't understand mental illness always insist that they are. I walk one to two miles a day. I get sun and fresh air. I leave my house. I've started cleaning out the piles of crap that accumulated when I was too tired to work. I write. I go to sleep before two a.m. I've stopped drinking and am training for a marathon. HAHAHAHAHA. Okay, not that last sen-tence. If I ever exchange vodka for running-on-purpose it'll be a pretty good sign that I'm in a cult and need rescuing. But the other things are things I'm pretty proud of. Again, I don't think I could have done any of those things in the deep depression I was in, but I'm taking advantage of the fact that right now I can do them.

I still often feel like a failure. I still have dark days. I still have to avoid certain triggers. I still have massive problems with concentra-tion and memory and motivation. I'm still broken. I'm still me. I'm still looking for a way through. But I'm glad to have found a way that helped me if for no other reason than to reaffirm that there is hope. There is always hope.

TMS is not for everyone and is still really in its infancy in many ways. It doesn't always work, and when it does work it could stop working at any time and no one knows why. It's uncomfortable and time-consuming and expensive. But for me, it was so worth it. I was (and remain) very lucky.

Two Months Later

I have a friend who is in AA who talks about working the program . . . doing the steps you continually need to do to stay healthy . . . and I realized how much I relate to that right now.

TMS gave me a reset button but I still have bad days. I still feel myself dip back into that dark place. I have more tools now than ever, and that helps, but sometimes the only thing that I accomplish in a day is just surviving. It's both an amazing achievement and also tinged with shame, as you see others who seem to whiz past you as you barely tread water. Maybe they're treading water too. You can't tell. You're just trying to breathe.

Today is one of those days for me. I think it's the weather. It's dreary and rainy and my joints hurt and it makes me not want to get out even though my doctor prescribed walking thirty minutes a day to keep my depression at bay.

It's part of my program. Today I took Hailey to school and then I went back to bed and stayed there until noon. I didn't enjoy it. People without depression won't understand that, but the fatigue of mental illness makes your very body a prison. The bed smelled sour. I couldn't concentrate on reading. Victor is out of town so I have no one to make me get up.

But I have to work the program. So I got up. I walked in the cold for ten minutes. Then I did another ten. Then I hit thirty. I brushed my teeth and took a shower. I brought my light therapy lamp out of storage. I wrote this post.

This is a good day. As far as mental illness is concerned, that is. I got out of bed. That in itself is pretty amazing. It doesn't always happen. But today it did and I'm proud of that. I will continue to work my program.

It's a program I add to all the time, finding tools that work for me. I share them with others. Others share with me. We get along. Together.

And alone.

So today I'm sharing some of my steps. I'm not sharp enough to think of them all but for now I'm writing them down to remind myself that I'm worth following them.

1. Follow your doctor's orders. For me that means anti-depressants and behavioral therapy.
2. Exercise thirty minutes a day, six days a week.
3. Get sunlight, or if you can't, use light therapy. Do not overuse your light therapy lamp even though you want to.
4. Treat yourself like you would your favorite pet. Plenty of fresh water, lots of rest, snuggles as needed, allow yourself naps.
5. Avoid negativity. That means the news, people, movies. It will all be there when you're healthy again. The world will get on without your seeing it.
6. Forgive yourself. For being broken. For being you. For thinking those are things that you need forgiveness for.
7. Those terrible things you tell yourself? Can you imagine if the person you love most were telling themselves those

things? You'd think they were crazy. And wrong. They think the same about you. Those negative things you are thinking are not rational. Remember that depression lies and that your brain is not always trustworthy.

8. Give yourself permission to recover. I'm lucky that I can work odd hours and take mental health days but I still feel shitty for taking them. Realize that sometimes these slow days are necessary and healthy and utterly responsible.

9. Watch *Doctor Who*.

10. Love on an animal. Go adopt a rescue, or if you can't, go to the shelter and just snuggle a kitten. Then realize that that same little kitten that you're cradling isn't going to accomplish shit but is still wonderful and lovely and so important. You are that kitten.

11. Get up. Go brush your teeth. Go take a hot shower. If you do nothing else today just change into a new pair of pajamas. It helps.

12. Remember that you are not alone. There are crisis lines filled with people who want to help. There are people who love you more than you know. There are people who can't wait to meet you because you will teach them how unalone they are. You are so worthy of happiness and it will come.

I feel weird about publishing a list of things that worked for me, because everyone is different and what works for me might not work for you. Hell, what works for me now might not work for me in the future. There are no promises with chronic mental illness. But still, I'm sharing this in the hopes that it helps. And I suppose that's another step. Trust in your words, even when you second-guess them.

Sorry this is so rambly. It's the best I can do. And that's okay.

Six Months Later

It's been half a year since I finished TMS. I needed less and less Xanax and haven't had any in six months. My depression was better for a while but lately I've had some hard days.

My depression has come back fairly often in the last half year but never lasted for more than a few days. This week was different . . . longer and darker. I'd blocked out how bad things were before TMS but suddenly I remembered it all. It was hard enough that I called to see about getting booster treatments. I'm not sure if they'll work but this isn't uncommon. Nothing lasts forever. The good and the bad.

This is the face of a woman who sometimes fears the mailman but who somehow conquered Europe. (And by "conquered" I mean "left the house and visited for about a week," which is a very big deal for me.)

TMS seems to have shocked me out of my lowest lows and it's good to know that it will probably be there when things get dark again. I hoped that would be farther off but I'll take it . . . that borrowed half year where I came back to life. The week after treatment I saw Europe for the first time.

I ate haggis and crepes (not together). I got lost in the catacombs under Paris. I fed dead chickens to owls in a haunted castle like some kind of terrible wizard. I saw the ravens at the Tower of London. I was there when my daughter gasped in awe the first time she saw the Eiffel Tower lit up against the starry sky. I hiked through mountains and slept on night trains and laughed with my family and explored strange, magical places so far from anything I'd ever thought I would see.

It was worth it. I am so lucky. I make the call. I keep the appointment. I work my program. This is the never-ending work of recovery.

I continue my journey.

The Golden (Shower) Years

When my daughter was little she'd ask me to tell her stories of what my childhood was like and I would tell her about the olden days of the eighties when cartoons only came on on Saturday morning and you couldn't watch *Alvin and the Chipmunks* because it was your sister's turn to pick one of the three channels and she wanted to watch *Muppet Babies*.

Hailey would look at me in awe. "And you couldn't afford YouTube?" she'd ask. And then I'd explain that there was a time before YouTube and then she'd start to doubt the veracity of my stories and I'd just say, "Yeah. We couldn't afford YouTube."

And it's not really a lie because even if YouTube *had* existed we wouldn't have been able to afford it.

We couldn't afford central heating either, so on cold winter mornings my little sister and I would often wake up with our clothes laid out on the bed the night before as extra blankets, dress under the warm blankets, and then race from our beds to the small kerosene heater in the living room.

If you've never been poor you maybe don't know what a kerosene heater is, so I will try to explain. It's a metal box the size of a large microwave that you pour kerosene into and then light it on fire. If you accidentally touched it you would be scarred for life because its metal surface was the temperature of the inside of a molten Hot Pocket, but the heat it gave out only extended about a foot and then inexplicably stopped entirely. Lisa and I would pull the kerosene heater as close as we could to the foot of the couch and huddle together on the floor, using the back of the couch as an ineffective coat. I'm pretty sure the only times we ever stopped fighting were when we were huddling for warmth, reading our books by the glow of the kerosene, careful to not put the heater close enough that it would start to melt the fake leather of the couch, which happened often enough that the smell of melted Naugahyde still makes me think of Christmas. We spent many winters in front of that heater, reading books that were often catching on fire and getting terrible sunburns on our shins and faces. Wealthier children got winter sunburns from ski vacations. We got ours from kerosene and poverty.

We had to be very careful not to accidentally bump into the kerosene heater because the tiniest jiggle would trigger the automatic safety shutoff and it could not be relit without matches, which our mother had had the great foresight to hide from us. Those were cold mornings, but nothing compared to the time we accidentally locked ourselves out of the house early in the morning (our parents had left for work hours earlier). It was freezing and our coats were locked inside, so we walked down the street to our school, but it was still dark and locked, and we huddled beside a storage building that blocked some of the wind as we impatiently waited for death. It's the coldest I ever remember being, and I thought this was a horrible way to die, wrapped around the very person who refused to let me touch her Strawberry Shortcake dolls.

I sort of wondered if my mother had somehow planned this. As if she'd said, "You girls will stop fighting *or I will make you hug each other until you die*."

Lisa and I bickered constantly but it wasn't really our fault. Living in a house with four people and one bathroom automatically meant you had to despise each other occasionally. It also meant you would love each other fiercely because you had no other choice. And sometimes it meant holding each other close as you waited for the sweet release of death. Or, in our case, for the elementary school receptionist to finally arrive and let us both in.

These were the dangerous days before cell phones. We relied on each other. For heat. For help. For life. And although my sister and I fought almost constantly, we are now the best of friends because no one else could understand the way in which we survived. And thrived. And lived.

Our kids know only that pressing a button brings heat (and a father who will tell them to stop messing with the thermostat and put on a goddamn sweater). They will never know the sort of cold that forces you into the bathroom to use a curling iron as a tiny heater to keep the feeling in your feet as you read and promise your mother that you really do have diarrhea this time. They will never know what it's like to cling to each other for basic warmth and comfort in the most human and desperate ways. And when Lisa and I relate these tales to them they look at us in horror and disbelief. I suppose we look at each other with a similar look. But ours is a bittersweet sadness that they'll never have those memories.

In retrospect, I can say those were good times, but probably only because retrospect allows you to not be there anymore. You get all the self-righteous feelings of living through your own weird personal hardships, such as "I Survived Sharing a Party Line with Everyone on My Block and That's Why Mrs. Williams and I Know All of Each Other's Secrets" and "All of My Mix Tapes Were Recorded Off of the Radio."

I suppose every generation has its own quirks. I'd often ask my great-grandparents to tell me about what it was like when they were little. My great-grandmother told me that during the Depression she and her brothers and sisters slept in one bed for warmth, and when one of them had to pee they'd just pee in the bed because otherwise they might freeze to death walking to the outhouse. I'm pretty sure this is worse than only having three channels, and I suspect she made it up to make me grateful for not getting peed on, but she seemed very authentic as she said, thinking back to the golden showers of her childhood, "Well, it was warm for a minute."

She told me those stories with love rather than anger or sadness, probably because she now was so distanced from them that they became sweet, rare memories. Of nonsexual golden showers. Memory is weird. As is perspective.

When Victor and I were first married we'd sometimes stay at my parents' in my childhood bed. It was the same antique bed my great-grandmother had slept in as a child and passed down to me, and as I'm writing this I just realized that it must have been the pee bed. It was very pretty, though, and I found it very warm, although Victor disagreed completely. By this time my parents had central heating but turned it off at night to save on the electric bill, and Victor would complain because he never understood how to use cats as heating pads. He never perfected the art of sleeping completely under the covers and letting your breath heat the homemade tent you created under the blankets. Eventually you either felt warm or you passed out from lack of oxygen. He also complained that the bed was uncomfortable and lumpy and felt like it was made of rocks.

"Don't be ridiculous. It's made of horsehair, I think," I said. "And also rocks," I admitted.

Then he looked under the bed and saw the stacks of large flat rocks keeping the mattress up. It made sense though, because the bed was over a hundred years old and the slats that made up the frame were cracked, so the flat rocks were necessary to keep the mattress supported. That bed had gone through so many deaths and births and everything else you could possibly imagine, so of course it needed rocks. For some reason Victor didn't find this reasoning comforting and refused to ever sleep in the bed again. He was like my own personal Princess and the Pea. Or Princess in the Pee, now that I think about it. At the time I thought he was being a bit snobby but I guess sleeping in a bed made of rocks and dead people's urine is asking a bit much if it's not something you're used to.

I think what I've learned from all of this is that even some of the worst experiences can be good so long as they didn't actually kill you. Even if you're in the worst situation ever, as long as it eventually ends, you win. The secret, I think, to a happy life is dying while you're up. Preferably in a warm bed unsupported by rocks with no one's pee in it but your own. In a room with a thermostat.

And all the eighties episodes of *Alvin and the Chipmunks* on YouTube.

And those bright, strange memories, which no amount of money could ever buy.

Awkwarding Brings Us Together

Not long ago I sent a small tweet out into the universe:

Airport cashier: "Have a safe flight." Me: "You too!" I CAN NEVER COME HERE AGAIN.

It was a tiny glimpse into the awkwardness of being me, but it set off a tsunami of responses that I still haven't entirely recovered from. Shockingly it was not from people telling me how stupid I am, but from people sharing how stupid *they* are.

Once high-fived a retail staffer who was helping me. Turns out she was waving to a friend outside the store. Still not over it. ~KIRSTENDUKE

I texted my boss at the end of my FIRST DAY on the new job with: "Heading out. Love you." Intended for my boyfriend. ~ANGEBASSA

An elderly man presented his discount card to me and I said, "You're getting ready to expire!" I could not recover. ~CRASHKRISPY

I talk fast and once told a customer at a bookstore that a new novel had made the "Man Licker Bonglist." #ManBooker-Longlist ~MISSLIBERTY

I had a cashier extend his hand slightly sideways and I shook it. He was asking for my coupons. ~LARAEAKINS

A friend's grandmother avoids funerals because instead of regrets she gets too nervous and congratulates the family. ~SLAYRAA

I once loudly proclaimed at work: "That's how the dildos went extinct!" Dodos. It was the dodos. ~BAD_GIRL_RISING

A friend thanks me for coming to their husband's funeral. My reply? "Anytime." ~CARDINALBIGGLES

Thousands of people sent me confessions of mortifying encounters they'd had with family or friends or total strangers. And then thousands of people read those stories and shared the horrifyingly embarrassing thing that *they'd* been carrying around all their lives. And it was glorious.

I recently answered a coworker's "How are you?" with a weird Chewbacca-like groan and was too embarrassed to fix it. ~SoxGirlNV

Noticed a blind man approaching me wasn't sure where I was so called out 'on your right.' I was on his left. He corrected me. ~TANYAPHILLIPS18

The cashier said "hi" to me and I said "Artichokes" because that's what she was holding. ~JAYELLEMO

My coworker asked what I was eating for lunch. I told her placenta. I meant polenta. :/ ~HOPEOR

Sent a female coworker an email attachment with "Here you ho" instead of "here you go." Twice. ~RINDSAY

My carry-on got pulled for a random search by the TSA. I had packed it so tight I warned the officer that "it might explode." ~THEARETICAL

I once accidentally texted my boss a soundclip of me flushing a toilet. ~ATINYBUN

At Funeral
Me: Sorry to hear your father was sick.
Friend: Thanks.
Me: Was it serious?
Friend: Yes, you're at his funeral. ~JAMESSPIRO

I went to mass. Guy in front turned around and said, "Peace be with you." I replied, "Pleased to meet you" and shook his hand. ~EDITOR_JAMES

The more stories that came in, the more I could relate to. And I wasn't alone. Most people laughed and cringed along with the confessors until they found the ones that resonated with them and responded, "OMG I DID THAT TOO ONCE AND LET ME TELL YOU HOW IT WAS EVEN WORSE."

Someone asked at my wedding if we planned kids soon. I got rugrats and ankle biters mixed, and said "Me? With rug munchers?" ~THEWILDGOOSE

New neighbors. Saw their wedding photo and said "Don't you miss the 80's?" They replied, "That was last year." It was 2005. ~LOU_C69

My junior prom, my date (now hubby) bought me a HUGE wrist corsage. I put my arm on our groups table and said, "Smell my bush!" ~MEG_1970

A friend went and placed her order at drive thru. She then heard "Could you drive up to the speaker? You're talking to the trash can." ~GOTCOOKIES

At hairdresser appointment, when asked what I wanted done I said, "Wash, cut, and a blow job." #horror ~MARISABIRNS

Mom told some people that I loved my Silver Bullet, which is a vibrator. She got the name wrong; it's a Magic Bullet blender. ~NATAGIRL3

Got into the passenger seat of the wrong car outside Starbucks. The driver waited until I finished my phone call to tell me. ~PARENTLIKEADAD

I pulled out a panty liner instead of a $5 bill to pay for my lunch. ~TAMBONE41

In public bathroom with my sister and while on toilet I reached under stall divider, grabbed her ankle to scare her. Not her. ~RAISINGPKS

And as these strangers shared the mortifying stories that had haunted them during sleepless nights at three a.m., they suddenly felt celebrated rather than ashamed as their unique, ridiculous tales brought people around the world laughter. The terrible details only made the stories more human and perfect.

The handsomest man I've ever seen once sat down next to me and said "Hi." I responded with "I'm eating a tootsie roll." He left. ~DAIZE_PLAYS

Grandma sees my big barreled curling iron and asks why I leave my "lady agitator" lying around for everyone to see. ~ITSGOTMYLEG

I went to the movie theater and asked for popcorn and Reeses Penises. ~JENNSASBRUINS

Pulled in to a gas station & was on wrong side of the pump for my gas cap. Drove around to the other side and did it again. Drove away. ~SKIMBLECAT

As a doctor I have on far too many occasions knocked on the door as I am LEAVING the room. ~DOCHOCSON

Working at a hardware store, picked up the intercom phone, forgot what I was doing and loudly said, "Hello?" to the entire store. ~ALIOFFTHEMARK

First date. Never eaten pistachios before. Crunched into a handful, shell and all. Pretended that's how I preferred them. ~FALLENPIXEL

I called my 9th grade crush and sang Happy birthday over the phone. When I finished his dad says, "Heath isn't here." ~SOUNDCHECKMAMA

I was looking for clip on sunglasses to go over my prescription glasses. Asked the pharmacist at CVS if they sold "strap-ons." ~RDWEATHERLY

Mistook the man limping toward me for someone I knew. "My god! What happened to you?" "I had polio as a child." I ran away. ~LUCYUNDERSNOWE

And as the stories continued to flood in I watched people slowly realizing that no one really wants to celebrate the size of your yacht/hair/waist/penis. What really brought the world together was dropping the pretense that everything is shiny and perfect so that, for a moment, we could all accept how wonderfully human we are.

I frequently wait for stop signs to turn green. ~AEGTX

We have a Texas sage plant that flowers before rain. When asked if it would rain today I said, "Not according to my bush." ~JE551CAW

Sandwich shop cashier: "What's your name?" Me: "Oh, uh, I have a boyfriend." Cashier: "For the sandwich." ~GROK_

At the dermatologist, my nurse asked if I needed anything else—I inexplicably said, "A CHRISTMAS HUG." Never went back. ~DIANEWADE3

Scooping ice cream one time a frozen shard of strawberry went under my thumb. It bled. I stabbed myself. WITH ICE CREAM. ~IMAGIN8ION

Was giving someone a Brazilian wax, and inadvertently glued my bangly bracelet to her labia. ~MARTINIFONTAINE

At museum, there was a section on animal lactation. Sneak up on sister and whisper in her ear canal, "Haa! Animal tit milk." Wasn't my sister. ~EMSBUM

Chatting with new neighbor. Spider crawls in my bikini top. Scream "Get it off!" and RIP OFF my top! Flashed 6 people. ~UNSEELIEME

Forgot word for teeth upon meeting hot dentist. "Can you fix my mouth bones?" ~ELPHRAT

Surviving mortification makes you stronger and more resilient because you have no other choice but to move on. Either you can let it eat at you, or you can celebrate it and bring joy to someone else who will cringe and giggle like mad along with you. Accidentally making shit awkward is such a familiar, vulnerable, and underrated accomplishment.

Warned coworker about creepy man lurking in the parking lot. It was her husband. :-/ ~KCLeventhal

Had a bagger help with my groceries. Couldn't remember where I parked. Looked around the whole lot before remembering I walked. ~Heading_West

I once got into the wrong car and tried for several minutes to start it. I left my cell phone there. ~CBTman

Had my laptop hooked up to a projector for a work meeting w/ execs, received an email from a friend: "WHAT THE FUCK IS RHUBARB" ~emmysuhweeks

Husband discreetly spit gristle into napkin. Waiter picks up napkin with flourish; gristle takes flight, lands on another table. ~NightOwly

Bought new dress for grandma's funeral; arrived, cousins shocked, laughing; grandma has on same dress. ~desert_flowers

Used to work at Home Depot & came across a man looking at paintbrushes. Need a hand? I said. He turned. He was missing a hand. ~_rallycap

As a teen writer I dabbled with "erotica." Hid the handwritten sheets inside stuffed toy. Mom gave away toy to neighbor kid. ~RIKITIKITALLIE

First gyno appt with my mom's doctor. During exam he said I looked like my mom. I asked if that was common. He meant my face. ~LWMALLARD

Days after I wrote my initial tweet the responses were still rolling in. It got so much attention that the *New York Times* wrote an entire article about it. Socialites and millionaires spend their entire life trying to get mentioned in the *Times* and turns out what really appeals to people are true stories of fucking up in incredibly human ways. To this day I can't read these responses without cry-laughing.

Nanny job interview, told job would involve light housekeeping. Replied: "I've never kept a lighthouse before but willing to try." ~GLENHA

Trying to be inconspicuous, hid tampon in sleeve headed to bathroom, waved hi to someone and it flew across floor. Kept walking. ~KARENSMITH_0808

Emailed the entire company I work at with the subject line "Cock In/Cock Out Report" instead of "Clock In/Clock Out Report." ~MARICBECKER

Farted very loudly w/coworker right outside my office. Picked up my cell and pretended it was my dad and farts were his ringtone. ~Mama_Cougar

While at the boat harbor I saw a jellyfish and screamed, "Look at those testicles!" as a fisherman walked by. Tentacles. Tentacles. ~EMILY_FORD

While we had company over, my son toddled down the stairs swinging my corded vibrator like a nunchuck. ~VULGAR-HOUSEWIFE

When "Stacy's Mom" song first came out, asked friend's roommate Stacy if her mom had it going on. She had recently died. So no. ~BEEGIBS

Paid in cash at Starbucks. Employee extends his fist, so I gave him a fist bump. Turns out he was just holding out my change. ~MARLAERWIN

And *this* is what humanity is made up of. Not saving orphaned otters from fires or flashy Instagram celebrities. It's made of unexpected farts and acute awkwardness and mortifying accidents and horrifying autocorrects. It's made of the very things that only humans can truly pull off. *And it's amazing.*

In college bio class, I SWORE I had seen a documentary on silicon-based life forms. Turned out it was from the X-Files. ~KBSPANGLER

Girl in next stall started talking to me so I kept chatting. Heard her say "Someone keeps talking to me." She was on the phone. ~SAMPLEHAPPINESS

Fell while working out. Skidded across the floor, rolled on my side and yelled, "Paint me like one of your French ladies." ~SCRAMBLEDMEGS91

Standing in line at a funeral, sweet old couple behind me, and my skirt just . . . fell off. To the ground. For no reason at all. ~BRIANNASHRUM

Asked my church to pray for a friend of a friend who lost his leg in an IUD explosion. I meant IED. Oops. ~MAMA_BEAR113

Tasting beers at a brewery. Poured ones I didn't like into a bucket like at wine tasting. It was their tip jar. ~MRROSTI-POLLO

Sent a corporate email apologizing for the incontinence instead of inconvenience. Signed it Satan, instead of Sara. ~SARAMARKS18

Passed bad gas alone in copy room at work. THEN coworker walked in. Blamed smell on radiator. Coworker calls maintenance. ~TWITWITTYVAL

Waiting while husband was using a port-a-potty, two city workers pick it up and start walking away. Too shocked to say he's inside. ~STEPHANIEARNOT

Me: Called the Dr and said I need to make an appointment with the VAGINACOLOGIST. Receptionist: laughing. Me: hangs up. ~SAYSOMSACK

Here's what I've learned: Whenever something truly mortifying happens, you have a choice. You can let it haunt you for the rest of your life or you can celebrate it, as today's awkward moment is tomorrow's fantastic story.

Your mortifying story will invite other people's stories into your world, and then suddenly there are so many of us sharing horrifying confessions that the people who don't have awkward moments are suddenly the awkward ones and for once, we—the artless misfits— can all feel a little sorry for them as they will never join this strange community or know our secret handshake. (By the way, our secret handshake = when someone waves at you and you go to wave back but then you realize they were waving at the person behind you but then they feel awkward and try to cover it by high-fiving you but you miss their hand and accidentally high-five them in the boob and then everyone runs away quickly and *we never speak of it again*.)

Ate a cookie on display in Anthropologie. Halfway through, realized it was a decorative soap. I finished eating it anyway. ~JUDICUTRONE

At a friend's dad's funeral I asked how her mom was, forgetting I'd been to that funeral six months before. Her response: "Still dead." ~ALISSASKLAR

Waved at a guy in a garden wearing sunglasses and a hat many times in passing over a weekend w/o responses. It was a scarecrow. ~FERNDALYN

In line at grocery store. Me: "Tell the nice man goodbye!"

Look down; realize I didn't bring the kids to the store.
~HATTIECHICKEN

Asked pharmacist if I could get some euthanasia for a cold
that won't go away. She said that seemed drastic. #Echinacea
~RACHNYCTALK

Presented myself: "Hi, I'm Ramona." The other person said,
"We have the same name" . . . My answer was, "Awesome,
what's your name?" ~RAMONABRUTARU

I once tried to remove a stray hair from the collar of a cute
guy sitting in front of me. Turns out it was attached to his ear.
~JUNEBUGSMUMMA

So the next time you do something incredibly embarrassing,
please remind yourself that you are being the most human you possibly can be and you're giving witnesses permission to forgive themselves for all the future embarrassment that lies in store for them. I
thank you for it. In fact, next time you do something mortifying you
can tell everyone that you did it for me and technically that means
it's all my fault. *EVERYONE WINS.*

Startled by "spider." It was a tomato top. Go to pick it up,
ACTUAL SPIDER RIGHT BEHIND IT, screamed and fell
over backwards. ~RUBYDEUCE

On phone to my bf on train, panicked: "Sorry I have to go, I
can't find my phone." Him: "How are we talking?" ~KASTREL

Gave waiter what I thought was a Groupon and got huffy when he said, "We don't take these." Was a recipe for turkey casserole. ~SASHATROSCH

I called my husband in a panic because I saw a van like ours in an accident. He said, "You're driving the van." ~DJS613

Thought my 4yo was next to me; instead told elderly man: "Hold my hand while we go down the escalator." Him: "Well if you insist." ~SUZDAL92

Nursing baby on British train. Smile at red-faced guy beside me. Notice baby is asleep. Boob is now resting on dude's forearm. ~BREEDEMANDWEEP

Responding to text message from my boss, I tried to write "Thanks so much" but after not typing perfectly it autocorrected to "Thanks douche." ~JULSHAZE

Told my friends that the guy in the car next to me was hitting on me. He was an undercover cop motioning me to put my seat belt on. Got a ticket. ~RYKATULRI

I couldn't remember the word "rhinoceros" so I called them "purple unicorn hippos." I haven't lived it down yet. ~MISPLACEDYANK

I told the hairdresser I wanted a "blunt cut" but moved the N to the second word. Said it three times. ~ROSEBURGIAN

Thought I was applying chapstick from my pocket. I just put a tampon to my mouth in front of a car sales showroom of people. ~RADIOLADIOROBIN

If you have managed to read these wonderful confessions without doing that thing where you're giggling so much people are staring and so you try to explain to them what's so funny but you're cry-laughing so hard that you can't get it out and they just stare at you like you're insane and that somehow makes it worse and so you laugh harder and then you get mad that they aren't appreciating how fantastically wonderful it all is, then we can't be friends, and honestly, I'm a little embarrassed for you.

That Time I Got Haunted by Lizards with Bike Horns

This morning began with me trying to save the world and Victor yelling at me for being *too* caring.

Victor is not pleased with this characterization because he says that today actually began with his slipping on the half of a Hot Pocket I left next to his car tire. This is technically true. But it's also true that I only left the Hot Pocket there to lure an owl into the garage so I could befriend it. Technically it's not legal to make owls into pets in America, but America isn't going to tell me who I can or can't be friends with and this particular owl seems really into it. I've named her Owly McBeal because she's a bit too thin (hence the Hot Pocket) and also because she seems feisty and able to handle herself in a court battle. Victor is not a fan because I guess he's threatened by strong women, and also because he says owls don't eat Hot Pockets and would make terrible pets that would probably carry away all of our cats and angrily chew on the clothed taxidermied mice on my shelves while staring at me in disgust.

These sorts of arguments are old hat for us. I grew up with my father rehabbing bathtubs of orphaned raccoons or diseased foxen. I'm perpetually always about to rescue an angry ferret or a sack of sick chipmunks. Recently I saw a poster of a fundraiser for a primate rescue sanctuary and on the poster was a drawing of a monkey wearing roller skates. And I was like, "Yes please. I *totally* want to roller-skate with a monkey. What is your adoption process?" but then when I reached out the sanctuary was like, "We're not open to the public, and also you absolutely cannot roller-skate with the monkeys. We have that on our sign because we have lots of famous former monkey stars that we rescued from exactly that sort of terrible existence." And I felt happy for the monkeys but also a little torn, because *what if they liked roller-skating? Roller-skating is awesome.* And now you have dozens of bored monkeys who never get to follow their passion. I offered to buy child-sized roller skates for the monkeys that we could leave out just in case the monkeys were into it and wanted to strap them on themselves, but the people still weren't having it. So instead, I found their Amazon wish list and I sent them a disco ball, because apparently monkeys love disco. Victor was like, "Why is there a disco ball on the credit card?" and I said, "It's not for me. It's for some famous retired monkeys who aren't allowed to roller-skate anymore." And that's when Victor threatened to turn off my credit cards.

If you listened to Victor you might think it's always been like this: me, the inveterate lover of weird animals that might chew your face off if given the chance; him, the grouchy misanthrope keeping homeless otters out of the pool. But it wasn't always that way. In fact, he is responsible for a number of questionable animals in our lives, including four before we were even married.

One

When Victor and I first started dating we were in college and he'd come to my house every night. I had a five-foot python named Stella that my dad had brought home as a surprise (surprise?). But Stella ate live rats and I couldn't handle that, so my dad would go to the pet shop once a week and get an elderly feeder rat to toss into Stella's tank and I would avoid thinking about it as I hypocritically ate bacon by the pound. My dad told Victor to come watch Stella stalk her prey, and Victor was still trying to impress my dad so he did, but the giant, fat white rat they tossed into the aquarium just sat up on his hind legs and his pudgy belly covered his feet completely as he glared at everyone like a furry Weeble Wobble. Stella crouched in the corner and my dad checked back every hour or so, but the rat's demeanor was just too intimidating. Stella seemed ashamed of herself, and the rat was walking all over her (literally), so my dad decided to pull the rat out and put it in the freezer so Stella could eat it later, because apparently if you leave a rat in with a disinterested snake, the rat will eventually attack it, like David and Goliath, and I was like, "*No.* This rat has been through enough. He goes free," and Victor and my dad both rolled their eyes at each other and my dad pulled the rat out by his tail so he wouldn't get bit, but this rat was super obese and old and that's why the rat's tail *CAME OFF IN HIS HAND*.

My dad was like, "Oh no," as he held a disembodied tail in his hand and the rat looked at him like, "*What (and I can't stress this enough) the fuck, asshole?*" and I said, "THAT'S IT. THIS RAT GETS A PARDON. THE RAT GOES FREE."

I scooped the rat into an empty cereal box as Victor tried to explain the circle of life to me but I wasn't having it. I drove to the bayou a few miles away as Victor looked at the fat rat bulge at the bottom of the cereal box.

"You are too stupid to be afraid of snakes," Victor said to the rat in the sort of voice you use when you're talking to babies you don't like. "Aren't you? Who's the stupid rat?"

A small squeak came from the box.

Victor stared at me in shock for a second and then quickly looked back into the box.

"Did you . . . did you just squeak at me? Did you?" His voice changed to the one you use when a dog smiles at you. "*Well, hello there, Squeaker. How are you? Who is the big boy talking to me? Is it you? It is you!*"

This is when we switched personalities completely and Victor made me drive back home to get three slices of cheese so that Squeaker would have a prepper stockpile in the wild. We tipped the box over at the bayou and I expected the rat to run from the people who had just tried to feed him to a snake, but instead he sat up on his hind legs and looked at us like, "So, why are we here? *This is a terrible party.*" Victor was like, "What is up with this rat? He thinks he's people," and I yelled, "RUN FREE, SQUEAKER," and eventually Squeaker gave us a shrug that seemed to say, "Whatever, weirdos," and he slowly waddled away into the weeds.

The next day at college Victor was like, "I wonder how Squeaker is doing," and I didn't have the heart to point out that it's probably pretty mean streets out there for an elderly white rat with a beer belly. I had another class to run to but Victor said he'd meet me at my house so we could do something later. On the way there though he stopped at the bayou, got out of his car, and looked around for a minute before yelling, "Squeaker!"

And that fucking rat wobbled out of the weeds and sat right the fuck on Victor's foot.

True story.

Victor scooped him up in his bare hands and carried him off to my house, and when my mom answered the door he looked absolutely pitiful as he cradled a balding, fat, nonplussed rat in his arms and said, "Can we keep him?"

Honestly, if *anyone else* had asked her, my mom would have said, "Oh *hell* no," but it was the first time he'd ever asked for something from her, so she sighed and shrugged and that's how Victor became a father. And Squeaker, our first real rescue pet, lived happily with us until he died of old age a few years later. Technically, I guess we rescued him *from* us, but I think it still counts as a rescue on the whole.

Some people might say that it was probably just another rat that was simply looking for an easy mark and maybe Victor was some sort of terrible Pied Piper, but there aren't a lot of fat white rats missing half a tail in our neighborhood, so I doubt it.

> **Sidenote:** *I realize this story sounds ridiculous, but weird animals adopt people all the time in insane ways. One time my uncle was in his backyard and turned around to find a bug-eyed parrot quietly stalking him. He followed my uncle around the yard for thirty minutes like he'd found his mother, and when my uncle tried to shoo him away the bird smiled enormously and screamed, "WHAT UP, TAQUITO!" He followed my uncle inside the house and when no one responded to the "DID SOMEONE LOSE A PARROT?" signs he put up in the neighborhood, Taquito became my uncle's new life partner. Sometimes your pets find you.*

Two

When we were still dating, Victor developed an obsession with reptiles and would take me out driving at night to capture snakes sleeping on the hot asphalt of country roads. He'd play with them for a bit and then release them back into the wild. One was a huge rat snake (named Paul) who was thin and needed rehabbing, so Victor tamed him and brought him to our friend Candy, who was afraid of snakes but wanted to care for one to break her phobia. Candy was in her fifties and was best known for chain-smoking, cursing, and her recurring catchphrase, "Look what you did to me, fucker," which she would say every time you made her get goose bumps from happiness, fear, excitement, etc. The first time Paul saw Candy she was wearing earrings that I guess looked like mice, because Paul immediately launched himself out of Victor's arm and bit Candy right on the face. Rat snakes don't have fangs but I still almost passed out, and Paul wouldn't let go of Candy's cheek even with Victor pulling on him, and I started to worry that it was going to be like those snapping turtles that only stop biting when lightning strikes them. Candy stared at Victor with a snake stuck to her face and said, "Look what you did to me, fucker."

She and Paul became best friends because after being bitten in the face she realized that it didn't hurt and it cured her of her phobia of snakes. It also started my phobia of watching people get bitten in the face by snakes.

Three

Not long after the Squeaker incident, Victor adopted a half dozen Tokay geckos (which were these giant, squicky lizards that crawled up the aquarium walls with their sticky, wet feet).

His resident advisor wouldn't let them stay in the dorm so Victor brought them to my bedroom. He set them up in a tank. He assured me that they wouldn't bother me at all and that he would bring them bugs to eat. It probably would have been fine except that every night I would wake up to a baby crying, and I didn't have a baby, so I was pretty sure it was a ghost baby calling for La Llorona. Also, it sometimes sounded like bike horns or someone throwing a rubber chicken, and that would set the ghost baby off again, and I thought I was going mad. I asked Victor to come over and bring holy water for a séance but after a few minutes he was like, "Oh, that's the lizards. Did I not tell you that they bark?"

No, reader. He did *not* tell me that the nocturnal, sticky-footed lizards in the tank next to my pillow "barked." He also didn't tell me that the tank they were in was infested with crickets and beetles who made their way out of the tank and all over my room and would hold screaming matches with the lizards at night like angry, battling picketers, if the picketers also had disgruntled babies with bike horns. It was the "Dueling Banjos" of the animal kingdom. And this is when I made him give back the lizards. Unfortunately, before I realized that the lizards were the ones fucking with me, I let one of them roam around my room free so that he could kill the escaped bugs, so even when Victor found a new home for the lizards there was still one crying bike-horn ghost baby haunting my room in search of equally-loud-but-in-a-different-way insects that I was afraid would crawl into my ear holes while I was sleeping. I'm just now wondering if this was Victor's plan all along, because within a few weeks he convinced me to get an apartment with him to escape the terrible temporary haunted jungle that was now my bedroom.

Jenny Lawson

Four

We were joined in our new apartment by Dallas, the matted ball of pedigreed anger that was Victor's ex-girlfriend's cat. Dallas had been evicted from his last home after he'd physically assaulted every one of his roommates, who were all human and at least twenty times his size. He was Persian and solid white except for the sour-smelling black tears that dripped down his face, making him look like his mascara was perpetually running. He would growl at you if you did something aggressive like sit on the couch or make eye contact. Or breathe.

Dallas. (This is his resting bitch face, which always looks like he's just about to start a fire with his mind.)

One time Dallas was scratching up a chair and Victor was like, "Stop fucking up the furniture, dude," and Dallas reared up on his hind legs, meowled like a banshee, and charged at Victor, who literally RAN from a fluffy white ball and barricaded himself in our bedroom before realizing how mortifying it was to be a grown man with a black belt running from a tear-stained kitty who looked like Liza Minnelli.

Years later, we rented our first house, a small hundred-year-old home that seemed to have been decorated by psychopaths. Several of the rooms were painted floor to ceiling entirely in the color of dried blood. The foundation of the house had settled and drifted so much that when you placed a ball on the floor of the kitchen it would roll on its own down the hall, picking up speed as it bounced through the bathroom and stopping only when it came to the bright white carpet in the living room, as if kicked by a ghost child who was also stunned by the ridiculous impracticality of solid white carpeting.

By that time Dallas had mellowed a bit and would occasionally let me pet him, but he continued to hate all men and would growl at Victor anytime he touched me. He would regularly wake up to Dallas quietly growling and glaring inches from his face if he thought Victor was sleeping too close to me. It was a little like living with a jealous ex, and Victor would remind Dallas, "Dude, you're *MY* cat. *I'm* the one that rescued you," but Dallas would just bare his teeth and then his left fang would get caught in his lip and he'd snarl adorably/menacingly. "DESTROY THE PATRIARCHY!" he seemed to whisper. He was really ahead of his time.

One morning I woke up to discover a horrible smell. Victor was gone, Dallas was hiding under the bed, and the entire living room carpet had somehow become leopard-printed overnight. On closer inspection I realized that the circular brown spots all over the carpet were shit. Apparently Dallas had gotten into the trash sometime in the night and eaten a bunch of watermelon. I didn't even know cats liked watermelon, but I have since discovered that it's great for constipated cats because it works like a laxative in small amounts. In large amounts it causes a veritable cat shitsplosion. Dallas's ensuing diarrheal fountain had gotten stuck in his long white butt fur, which he'd attempted to clean by using the entire house as his own personal toilet paper. The white carpet was stamped everywhere with his shame. He'd also made use of the tile in the rest of the house as he dragged his ass in long calligraphy-esque smears, as if some sort of maniac were leaving me indecipherable but graceful cursive threats written in shit.

I spent the rest of the day scrubbing butthole smears off every surface of the house. I called Victor for backup but he informed me that he had seen the devastation when he left for work but he'd been running late and was sure I could handle it myself since Dallas was obviously *my* cat, after all. He was a coward, certainly, but in a way it was a team effort, because while he was gone I used Victor's towel to clean the floor and then shaved all the fur off of a miserable cat's butthole with his electric razor.

My point here is that I take a lot of shit (literally, it seems, in some cases) for being the person in our marriage who brings weird animals into our lives, but technically I'm just trying to catch up to all the strange animals Victor (and life) has thrown at me. In fact, just last week I got beaned in the head with a live squirrel, which seems like some sort of terrible message from God.

I assumed the squirrel fell out of a tall tree, and it hit me so hard I seriously worried that I had a concussion. I think a head injury from a suicidal squirrel would be a very embarrassing way to die but would at least give the CSI team a good mystery because THERE WEREN'T EVEN ANY TREES ABOVE ME. The squirrel was stunned for a few moments (*fucking join the club, sir*) and I thought I'd maybe found a new pet, but then he shook himself and loped away. I considered that maybe this was an elaborate failed murder scheme where the murder weapon runs off (and also is a squirrel), but later my dad told me that hawks and owls often pick up squirrels or snakes or other small snacks and fly off with them to their nests, but sometimes they lose them midair in the struggle and their dinner plummets back down to earth. I'm guessing this is why women in the Wild West always carried parasols. There were probably a lot more hawks and varmints back then, and getting beaned in the noodle by a squirrel was no picnic but I imagine having a bird drop a live angry snake on your head would *really* ruin your morning.

Victor has pointed out that the most likely culprit for the squirrel bombing is Owly McBeal, and he's probably right, but whereas Victor sees this as some sort of threat, I'm pretty sure that it's just her way of sharing her dinner to pay me back for all the snacks I've left out for her. It might also just be her way of telling me that she can't easily eat the bowls of leftover macaroni I leave out any more than I can eat a live squirrel, and that's precisely why I switched to Hot Pockets. After all, being smart enough to train me and caring enough to share snacks with me make excellent qualities in a pet.

I think perhaps life is all about dealing with whatever life throws at you. You can focus on cat diarrhea and missing tails and squirrel missiles, or you can celebrate the strange magic that brings the unexpected into your life and scritch sweet furry (or scaly) faces whenever you can. I know which one I'm choosing.

Now, if you'll excuse me, I have some tiny roller skates to throw over a chain-link fence.

We Are Who We Are Until
We Aren't Anymore

I love stories about my family. It's the reason I write mine down. I search them out from relatives and my sister and I compile scrapbooks with old pictures of ancestors we've never known and stories passed down through generations. Some of them are beautiful. Some are funny. Some are tragic. Some are lies. Some are lost.

I only discovered this when I started studying genealogy. I did DNA tests and joined ancestry websites where you can share information and find the stories that census forms and death certificates tell. Some people get into genealogy because they want to find their famous ancestors, but I already know this isn't likely for my family. We're mostly from farmers and peasants, but our stories are just as interesting if you can find them. My mother's ancestors came from Ireland and England but so long ago I only know that from our DNA tests. My father's family emigrated from Bohemia only a few generations ago, so anything before they sailed into New York is lost to me. If my grandparents were still alive I could ask them to translate the few Czech documents I've found, but they are gone, and so, unfortunately, are their stories.

Victor doesn't deal with all of this because 1) he doesn't care, and 2) one of his relatives already did his genealogy and found that he came over on the *Mayflower* and according to the records is a descendant of the Count of Worms (which is the most ridiculous title ever; I sort of love it). His family has an actual crest, which is of a swan pecking a bloody hole in its own chest to feed its babies with blood, with the words "DRINK OF ME AND LIVE FOREVER" under it, which is, first of all, *not how you feed swans*, and also sounds pretty vampiric if I'm being honest.

If my family had a crest it would probably be bad choices and tractors, which would actually make a pretty great country song now that I think about it.

The reason I started searching our family history, though, was because of my granny, my mom's mom. She is sweet, kind, and (sometimes unintentionally) hilarious. She also has dementia and for the last several years has been losing much of what makes her her. When she was first diagnosed she gave me and my sister her old photographs and told us the stories of her childhood so they wouldn't be lost. About her favorite days, when she was young and the farm work was done and she could pack a lunch and her gun and a book and ride her bike someplace quiet to read. About the time she had a fight with her sister Edie and buried Edie's china set and never (to that day) admitted that she'd done it. It's still buried at the farm.

One story she told a lot was about her great-grandmother. She hadn't really known her and her mother would become furious when Granny would mention her. According to family lore she was Native American and her husband (a circuit-riding reverend) traded a bunch of animal hides to her father for her. He died not too long after when his horse ran into a barbed-wire fence and then the unnamed woman disappeared.

Granny said that her sister had a birthmark on her back that looked like a bird, and Granny had one in the same place that looked like a bird with a broken wing, and when she mentioned the marks to her mother she told Granny to never speak of them again. Somehow, Granny thought, these things were connected. That perhaps the birthmark was a sign of belonging. I'm not sure if it was the beginning of the dementia or just her normal stubbornness but she became obsessed with it, and so my grandfather started researching it and my sister and I helped.

My grandmother's DNA test showed some Native American DNA but not as much as you'd expect; however, many Native Americans (understandably) don't want to share their DNA with large corporations, so there are some tribes and families that aren't really represented. I searched through the records and libraries for more than a year and I found the Native American ancestors who showed up in her DNA results. Often the records just ended with "unknown Cherokee woman" but sometimes I found fascinating stories, like that of my great-(x 8)-grandmother who was part of a Shawnee tribe until her parents were killed by a warring tribe. According to the records, she and her siblings were in danger of starving until they were adopted by the Cherokee Nation. And when I'd share those stories with my grandmother she always had the same response. "Well, goodness' sakes, Jenny-girl!" Then she'd pause for a second to digest it and ask if I'd found anything about her great-grandmother.

I had.

The problem was that the woman in the records was listed as white on the census forms. I found her reverend husband and his grave and discovered that she'd lost her property after his death when she couldn't find the deed to their land. Then she disappeared into another life. I found other people in the comment sections of genealogy websites (who were distantly related to me apparently) who expressed their confusion because they had also been told the same story as my grandmother.

I don't know the answer here. Maybe she was Native American but passed as white because of the racism of the time. Maybe the records are wrong. (They often are.) Or maybe she had another secret altogether and the rest of the family made up that she was Native American so that no one would mention her outside the family, lest they have to face the prejudices of that day. I haven't found the secret yet. I'm still searching.

But in my search I've found so many stories that make up the lives of my family, although they never tell enough.

One of the people whose story affected me the most was Lillie, my great-great-grandmother. I never knew her but when I was look-ing through her records I discovered that she'd died in the fifties in a mental institution not far from where I grew up. Her death certif-icate listed her cause of death as a heart attack but a contributing factor was "psychosis." I wondered how psychosis could cause a heart attack. I asked my mom but at the time stories like Lillie's were kept secret—something to be ashamed of—so Lillie's story is lost. But I did some research and found out about the treatments given at the institution at the time. There was electroconvulsive therapy, which is still practiced today with some great results, but at the time the therapy was experimental and often brutal. They practiced "fever" therapy, where the temperature of the patient was artificially raised to . . . I don't know . . . burn the crazy away? They practiced hydrotherapy, where patients were forcibly strapped into baths or sprayed with high-pressure hoses. They practiced insulin therapy, where patients were repeatedly put into diabetic comas over and over again. The treatments were extreme and in some cases barbaric, and many patients, like my great-great-grandmother, didn't survive them.

It wasn't that long ago that I would have been in that place, getting those treatments. I'm not, though, because of a number of things. Because treatment is better. Because doctors and scientists keep learning. Because mentally ill people have more options and more advocacy and so much of that comes from the fact that we are talking about this stuff now. Treatment isn't happening in dark rooms with no windows. We are so much less likely to lock away the people who suffer, and the stigma of mental illness is fading. Slowly. I can trace mental illness or mental disorders going back through four generations in my family. The illness isn't going away, but the treatment of it is getting better. It gives me hope, which is good because in looking through our family history I can see patterns that foretell a future that scares me.

Lillie's daughter (my great-grandmother) was kind and sweet and scrappy and eventually developed dementia when I was a teenager. She knew what she was in for. Her mother had battled mental illness. Her husband had been diagnosed with dementia years earlier and we had watched him slip away. Now their daughter, my wonderful grandmother, is in the same fog. If we live long enough, chances are it will catch my mother and then me. These are the patterns you see if you look hard enough.

My grandmother is in a "memory facility" now. It's nice, even resortlike, compared to the treatment her grandmother lived through. My mother visits her almost every day for hours at a time and she calls me at night to tell me what happened that day. We're lucky because Granny is lost a lot but she's still happy and cheerful and positive most of the time. In many ways she's become a child again, and my mother tells me that even though it's a terrible disease it has been strange and wonderful to get a glimpse into the past at what my grandmother was like as a child.

My grandmother attends church services and sings the songs she knew as a kid as loud as a child would. The attendant after the service says to her, "Joy, I know you like these peanut butter crackers so I brought you extras," and my granny beams and says, "Oh boy! I may not know my own name but I know I love these peanut butter crackers."

The laundry sometimes lost her clothes, so my mom bought her new ones and wrote her name and room number in red Sharpie in them so that they wouldn't get lost, and when my grandmother saw them she picked up the underwear with her name in it and said, "Oh how wonderful! Now when I forget who I am I can just take off my panties and hand them to a nurse and say, 'Here. This is who I am and where I belong.'" We think she was kidding.

She struggled at first with thinking that she'd lost her parents, or that she'd missed their funerals (she hadn't), but not long ago she quietly asked my mom, "My parents are dead, aren't they?" and my mom explained that they were in heaven watching her. She looked off and said, "I thought so. If they were alive they would have come to get me by now." And then Mom's heart broke a little and my granny laughed and said, "They're probably looking down at me saying, 'Girl, get your brains together!'"

The last time I saw her she didn't know who I was even when I told her, but she was still so happy to see me and she was aware enough about her condition to say to me in her heavy Texas accent, "Well, for goodness' sakes! I wouldn't know you if I'd run over you with my car." And then she laughed. And I laughed.

She's still in there, somewhere, but she drifts more and more. Yesterday she was playing bingo with my mom when suddenly she didn't understand what the letters were. Then she got quiet and a little scared and my mom said, "Let's go for a walk." They walked around the courtyard silently and after a while Granny said, "Oh, when did you get here?" And my mom told her about all that they'd done that day and Granny slowly nodded and said, "Oh, yeah. I think I went away for a little while."

"Yep," Mom said cheerfully. "But that's okay. You came back."

And they both laughed.

"But one day," my mom said to me later, "she won't come back."

It's true. She loses little pieces of herself and the ability to do the things that bring her joy. I discover new stories of our family on genealogical websites and I want to share them with her but I've waited too long. She can't concentrate in the abstract. But she loves the stories of her childhood, and she and my mom talk about the old farm and relatives long since gone. My mom tells her stories from their past, and Granny drifts in and out and sometimes thinks that my mom is her childhood best friend or tells stories about her mama and daddy as if they had just happened. And sometimes even those stories go away.

When I see my granny I sometimes wish I could catch up the pieces she drops behind and hand them back to her or keep them safe in my own head. But that's not the way it works. Instead I do what I can . . . I write down her stories and remember them for her and hope it's enough.

We are lucky that—for the moment, at least—my grandmother is cheerful in the face of adversity. She is strong and fragile. She is stubborn and demanding and sweet and hilarious and sad and confused. She is a concentrated version of who she always has been, someone who changed my life and who inspired me and still inspires me. She goes missing sometimes, lost in her own mind, but when she comes back she is still the same strong woman who proudly wears the birthmark of a bird with a broken wing.

I see the difference between the life she lives now and the one her grandmother lived through. And it gives me hope. We are getting better. Slowly . . . much too slowly. We are so far from perfect but we build on the shoulders of those who come before us and (*I hope, God, I hope*) we learn from them and we grow and evolve. Their stories push us forward in good and bad ways, but only if we are willing to listen.

INTROVERTS UNITE!
(But Sweet Baby Jesus, Not in Real Life.)

Someone once told me that the difference between introverts and extroverts is that introverts recharge by being alone (like any normal person) and extroverts recharge by being with others (like vampires). I live with two extroverts, which is helpful in that they keep me from becoming a complete hermit but also terrible because they have no concept of the utter emotional and physical exhaustion that comes from living in a world that is too peoply.

If you've ever been on the Internet you've probably taken bunches of "Are You an Introvert?" quizzes, but honestly it sort of feels like they never have realistic answers. So I've decided to make my own:

You're at a thrift shop with your husband and find an antique taxidermied alligator in a ballerina costume but there isn't a price. You:

A   Ask your husband to ask the price.

B   Get irrationally upset when your husband refuses to ask how much it is because "you already have too many dead alligators anyway."

C Cradle Allie McGraw in your arms as you walk through the store but then put her back on the shelf because you're too exhausted from even thinking about talking to the clerk and now you need to go home.

D Tell your husband to buy Allie McGraw for you because you (intentionally) forgot your purse in your car, and before he realizes there isn't a price tag tell him you have explosive diarrhea and run to the bathroom.

You've arrived at a party but no one you know is there yet. You:

A Request a great song and start a line dance.

B Find a dog to talk to.

C Have a fight with an imaginary person on your phone so that the strangers who haven't even noticed that you are there will think you have a good reason to leave.

D This is a trick question. You would never go to a party.

The person you had a crush on in high school gets behind you in line at the grocery store. You:

A Enthusiastically hug them and ask them why they weren't at the high school reunion that you organize every year.

B Give them a quick hi, then immediately pretend that you forgot to buy tampons and scurry away. Realize you just talked about tampons to your high school crush. Dump everything in the frozen food aisle and run away.

C   Burn the grocery store to the ground and then move to another state.

D   Not applicable since you have all of your groceries delivered so you don't have to leave the house.

No one calls your phone all day long:

A   That's because I called everyone first.

B   Maybe my phone is broken?

C   Good. Only monsters call when they could text.

D   My phone is just for downloading otter videos.

Your mail carrier rings the doorbell. You:

A   Answer the door. Duh.

B   Pretend to not be home unless they leave a note on the door that says they need a signature. If they do, quickly decide if it's harder to answer the door now or to go to the post office and talk to the clerk there.

C   Only psychos and murderers ring doorbells. Feel immediate dread and drop to the floor so they won't see you through the window. Remain there until you hear the mail truck pull away.

D   Trick question. You have disabled the doorbell and have a sign on the door saying that your rabid Rottweilers are sleeping and should not be disturbed.

When working in a group you think:

A   This is so much fun!

B   Let's divide up the work and meet back when we're done.

C　I'll just do it all.

D　YES OFFICER I'D LIKE TO FILE A COMPLAINT.

Your inner monologue is:

A　The more the merrier!

B　One good friend is gold.

C　My best friends are books and cats.

D　CAN I GET ONE GODDAMN SECOND ALONE, SUSAN?

Your dream vacation is:

A　A weeklong music festival of mosh pits and sleeping with strangers.

B　A week in the countryside with a few friends.

C　A week in bed with books and no judgment.

D　THIS QUIZ IS EXHAUSTING AND I RESENT HAVING TO ANSWER IT.

If you answered mostly A's: You are probably my husband.

If you answered mostly B's: You are the most dangerous kind of introvert: the functional introvert who sets an impossible standard for hermits. I still love you, but you are killing me.

If you answered mostly C's: There is room in my pillow fort for you. But mainly just because I know that you won't come.

If you answered mostly D's: You are me. Also, you are probably exhausted just from imagining these social situations, and I would like to invite you to my house and then immediately cancel so that both of us feel happy to have thought about being social without actually doing any of the work.

Introverts come in all degrees, and sometimes that can be confusing for others. Some are fine with other people but prefer alone time. Some can seem outgoing on the surface or have the ability to fake it for short periods of time. I am a super introvert, but on good days I can make myself take meetings or go to the store. I turn down invitations that other people would jump at. I only do interviews if they agree to do it by email because I know that talking on the phone with a stranger for even a half hour will drain me for the rest of the day.

I've lived in my town for five years and I have one friend. Not like one really good friend and a lot of acquaintances. I have *one* friend. I have never had a meal with another person who lives in this town that I wasn't related to. This might seem sad and lonely to some people, but actually I feel very lucky to have one person not related to me who truly understands when I text her at one a.m. about an anxiety attack and (if sober) will come over and watch bad reality TV with me for five hours straight while we drink box wine in our pajamas. One friend is a lot. It's one more than I've had at many times in my life.

In fact, there are periods in my life when the only close friend that I have is me. And that can be a bit sad during times when I am not someone that I even want to be with. But in some ways it's important. I am alone so often that I criticize myself and hate myself and love myself and get way too into my own head. It's why I'm a writer. Sometimes these essays are a way to reach out from the safety of my quiet room. Sometimes they are letters to myself. Becoming my own friend is hard and a struggle, but it's one of the greatest gifts you can give yourself. Becoming your own friend means taking care of yourself the way you would someone that you love. And that's hard. But it is necessary.

I think that we tend to judge ourselves by the parties we attend or the trips we take or the selfies we post . . . the ones where we don't look happy enough, so we take them again and again until we have that perfect forced pose that we hope shows strangers that we are not as alone as we fear we are.

Right now, as you read this, you are alone, you gorgeous solitary creature. But I am with you. We share this paragraph and these words, and even if you don't agree with me you are listening and we have connected in small and large ways. And in that way we are not alone. We are together.

And in a way that doesn't even require you to put on pants.

My Dentist Hates Me

"I've never had a cavity in my life," I proudly say to my dentist exactly thirty seconds before he informs me that I have two cavities.

I was not expecting this (not because I regularly floss—who has time for that?), because my previous dentist told me that I grind my teeth in my sleep (which was not a surprise as teeth grinding and anxiety are often two-for-one) and apparently I do it in a strangely beneficial way where I grind my teeth down *just enough* to grind out any cavities before they take hold. This year, however, the cavities won a race I didn't even know I was having with my teeth. I blame Victor, because he's constantly telling me to stop grinding my teeth, since I guess he'd rather have all my teeth fall out than listen to the sounds of my binge-eating dream macaroni in my sleep.

The dentist assured me that he could easily fill the cavities while I was there and I'm certain lots of people would be fine with that, but those are normal people who don't need to take Xanax to see a dentist and who didn't just learn that *someone was going to be drilling holes into their skull.*

Victor (who'd just finished his cavity-less cleaning and was sitting with me for mine) thought I was overreacting, but I keep my teeth in my skull so I'm pretty sure I'm right.

Frankly, I don't understand why they have to *drill* holes in your teeth to fix cavities, because cavities already are holes. Isn't the fact that there is a hole in my tooth the problem to begin with? It seems extreme and counterintuitive and I'm pretty sure it's some sort of pyramid scam to give me bigger and more expensive cavities. Victor tried to calm me down, assuring me that it wouldn't hurt and explaining to the dentist that I was just paranoid because I'd had a bad experience when I had my wisdom teeth removed a few years ago.

"Did you have complications?" the dentist asked me as he readied his equipment.

"Yes," I admitted. "My house was invaded by leprechauns."

"Good God," Victor said. "That is not true."

"Well, it sort of is," I explained. "The surgery was fine but the drugs made me really sick afterward, so when I got in the car to go home I threw up out the window and the dental assistant had to come out and change out my gauze in the parking lot while I acted like a total idiot. It was a lot like being back in college but with more dental assistants."

"Jesus Christ," Victor mumbled.

"But then I fell asleep when I got home and Victor woke me up at midnight to tell me someone was sneaking around our house. I was all, '*Something's sneaking around in our house? Like a leprechaun?*' and he was all, 'No, *drunky.* Someone's OUTSIDE the house,' and he grabbed the riot gun and ran outside. And I sat there thinking that he was never going to be able to shoot a leprechaun because those things are freaking *nimble*. So I find the phone and dial 'nine' and 'one' and decide to wait until I hear a gunshot before I dial the other 'one' and then I see Victor lugging in a giant box. Turned out that our neighbor signed for a package for us and was just leaving it on our porch. It also turned out that I'd pressed 'memory' and 'one' and so I accidentally left a very weird muttery message on my own voicemail about leprechauns."

Then Victor gave me that stare that means I should stop talking, but it was too late because I was fully into nervous rambling and I couldn't stop, so I decided to change the subject by asking the dentist if he had any extra human teeth that I could have.

In hindsight I realize this was not a great topic. But I explained that if I were a dentist I'd bury all the extra teeth I pulled in a pit in the backyard and then maybe a hundred years from now someone would dig them up and be like, "Holy crap! A serial killer must've been here!" And that would be nice because it's fun to add a little mystery to strangers' lives. I'm a giver.

I explained that a necklace of petrified ears would be even better, but the dentist stared at me and clarified that he doesn't remove ears (I know, dude. I was just making polite conversation). He told me that he couldn't give me a jar of strangers' teeth but that he had once known a dentist who made jewelry out of the teeth people didn't want to keep, and I thought I'd probably get along with that dentist. Except that we'd probably fight over the teeth.

I settled into the chair as the dentist began working, but it was uncomfortably quiet and I kept thinking of how much I didn't want everyone to just ruminate on serial killers and leprechauns, so I said, "So did you see those big balls in my mouth?"

The Novocain had already kicked in and my tongue was numb,

and also there was a hand in my mouth, so my dentist removed his hand because *clearly* he thought he'd heard wrong, and I said (loudly, to counteract the numb tongue), "I THAID, THID YOU SEE THE BALLS IN MY MOWF?"

(Let me just stop here to explain that this is *not* my fault. The dental hygienist had brought up my mouth balls during the cleaning so I assumed this was a normal dental topic, but clearly it is not. During my cleaning she'd done X-rays and she showed me a picture of the inside of my mouth that she found fascinating. On the lower part of your jaw—the part your tongue rests on—some people have these two round balls of jawbone. Run your tongue around your lower jaw. I'd always assumed everyone had these but she explained that few people grow these jawbone balls so they're always interesting to find. It's not a medical concern, and I found it sort of comforting because I'm pretty sure this proves I'm not overweight, I'm big boned. Literally. In the mouth.)

The dentist stared at me as he tried to decipher what I was saying and said, "Um . . . ?" and I looked at the dental hygienist for help and said, "The ballths in my mowf?" and pointed to my mouth while she stared at me in confusion and made me look even crazier than normal. Then she exclaimed, "Oh!" and said something in Latin that was either the technical name for the balls in my mouth or possibly code for "I think this bitch is crazy. Someone call security."

And then the dentist was like, "Oh, of course! Big balls in your mouth. Lemme see 'em." He peered under my tongue and said, "Oh yeah. Cool. There they are." He shrugged. "I've seen bigger."

It was a bit dismissive, and frankly I felt a little disappointed that he'd seen other people with more impressive balls in their mouths, but I figured maybe he was trying to make me feel like less of a freak and I took comfort in that. He explained that some people have such big balls in their mouth that they have to go to a professional to remove them, and that sounded a bit *too* intimate. I joked that the only thing I ever needed removed from my mouth was feet, and he looked at me strangely again, and Victor cleared his throat and hurried to pay. Now that I'm writing all this down I realize I should have said that I often need help removing *my* foot from my mouth because I'm always saying ridiculous things. Saying that I have to have help removing "*feet* in my mouth" makes me sound like some sort of foot-fetish deviant whose eyes are bigger than her . . . mouth? *Which sort of proves entirely my issue with putting my foot in my mouth.* Both to the dentist and to any foot-fetish people who now think I'm judging them: I'm totally not. More power to you. I'm not judging. Hell, I've got giant balls in my mouth. None of us is innocent here.

So long story short . . . I had two cavities today. Although technically I have lots of them because "cavity" is just another word for "hole" and my whole body is practically *filled* with holes. In fact, some of my favorite parts are holes.**** I guess what I'm saying is that maybe we should embrace our holes and stop looking to strangers to fill them, although I guess my dentist isn't really a stranger and I did pay him to fill my cavities and I should probably reword that because now I sort of feel dirty. Also Victor says that now we need to find a new dentist, but that's ridiculous, because the great thing about mortifying yourself in front of professionals is that there's no place to go but up and you don't have to worry about keeping up shiny, false appearances. It's almost impossible to do that with someone who has seen balls in your mouth. These are the basic life lessons no one ever teaches.

**** Specifically my ear holes. Get your mind out of the gutter, weirdos.

Am I Even Still Alive?

So I got a call from my doctor that I tested positive for tuberculosis, which was weird because I'd never even asked her if I had it and had no symptoms and I couldn't tell if she'd maybe gotten the wrong number or was just really, really good at her job.

"We need you to come in today so we can test you again," she said.

". . . To see if I have double tuberculosis?" I asked. "Jesus. This is getting worse by the moment." I considered hanging up before she told me that I was already dead, but she quickly explained that it might have been a false positive so I needed to be rechecked.

This is sadly not unusual for me. One of the side effects of having a collection of chronic diseases is that the treatments to keep the diseases at bay can sometimes be more harmful than the diseases themselves. When untreated, my rheumatoid arthritis is debilitatingly painful, and during flare-ups I end up in wheelchairs and emergency rooms. The pain is on par with childbirth, except that instead of getting a baby at the end you are treated like a drug addict as you demand the only narcotic you know will make the pain go away. I am quickly labeled a "drug seeker" (which is shorthand for "addict" in the ER), and it's hard to argue with that because I am seeking drugs, because I'm addicted to the sensation of not being in abject pain. I'm weird like that.

Several years ago I found a rheumatologist who told me that I didn't have to be in pain and started me on monthly biologic injections. They are crazy expensive and have a lot of risks and side effects, but I'm currently in remission from RA. I haven't been in a wheelchair or ER in years. I don't take any pain medication. Sometimes I wish I could go back to those ERs and show them that I was telling the truth and that I needed help rather than judgment, but I won't because I know they're just doing their job and also they might have filed a restraining order against me for things I said to them while in pain.

I'm incredibly lucky to have the medications available now, as my great-grandmother had RA and was wheelchair-bound at my age. But the medication isn't perfect and brings with it a lot of assorted bullshit. Last year I was diagnosed with medication-induced lupus, which is like regular lupus but you give it to yourself. I could have chosen to go off the meds but RA feels worse than medication-induced lupus, so I stuck with it. The medication also makes it hard to fight off all sorts of things, like tuberculosis, which is no picnic normally but super-duper deadly if you're on this medication. That's why the doctor checks my blood all the time and that's why I had to go in to see if I was dying from a disease I'd last heard of on *Little House on the Prairie.*

Victor offered precious little sympathy as he considered setting fire to all the parts of the house that I'd touched, so I texted a more sympathetic friend, who was all, "OMG, you have TB?!" and I was like, "Well that's what the bloodworm said," and she was like, "JESUS, YOU HAVE BLOODWORMS TOO? HOW ARE YOU EVEN ALIVE?" and I was confused for a minute until I realized that my phone had autocorrected "blood work" to something scarier than "blood work." But with my luck, yes, I probably have bloodworms too.

Small footnote that I'm not putting as a footnote because it's too long: Last year our whole family had to take medicine for buttworms because one of us was exposed to them so we all had to take this medicine to kill them. But I couldn't find the medicine anywhere and finally Hailey just went up to every pharmacist at every drugstore in our neighborhood asking for buttworm medicine because she's not even close to being embarrassed by buttworms—honestly I think she's adopted. And maybe you're reading this and judging us for having buttworms but first of all, most people with buttworms don't even know they have them, so you probably have them right now. They are shockingly common (in spite of the horrified look that several clerks gave us when asked about buttworm juice, which admittedly is a poor choice of words when describing the liquid medicine you have to take to evict buttworms). They're like the lice of the butthole and kids get them all the time. They're so common that when one person in your house is suspected of having them you just treat everyone because buttworms are fucking everywhere, apparently. Most of the time you don't even know because they usually stay up inside of you. I never saw any buttworms myself, but that doesn't mean anything because maybe my buttworms are just homebodies. Also you can't judge me for having buttworms because *I* don't have buttworms. Because I took the buttworm juice. This butthole is clean, thank you very much.

I don't know how we were exposed to buttworms in the first place but I blamed the cats, because those fuckers stick their butt-holes on every surface of the house, including your pillow and your keyboard, and if you don't think your cat does the same then you probably don't have a glass coffee table that you have to scrub butthole puckers off of every day. Butthole puckers are the sticky fingerprints of your pets. My doctor said that cats can get butt-worms but not the same kind that people get, which was sort of a relief because I didn't want to have to feed buttworm juice to three angry cats. It was bad enough having to tell Victor that he needed to drink the shot glass of buttworm juice, *which did not go over well* and resulted in his wanting to burn the house down, which is weird because they didn't live in our house, Victor. They lived in our buttholes.

Also, spellcheck keeps telling me that "buttworms" isn't a real word and I understand your disbelief, spellcheck, but just because we want them to not be real doesn't mean that they aren't.

Oh my God, I totally got distracted by my buttworms. Sorry. This chapter is not about buttworms. It's about tuberculosis. Which the doctor also said I didn't get from cat buttholes. In fact, she said it mostly comes from prisons and schools, which are pretty much the same thing if I'm being honest.

Sorry. Back to the TB.

I went to get more blood work and a chest X-ray but the nurse seemed a little frazzled at how many times she was sticking me and I assured her that this always happens as I have tiny, rolly veins, but that it was sort of a blessing because it probably kept me from doing heroin, and she breezily said, "Oh, you could find a way. If you really want heroin you can make it work," and I was like, "Are you giving me a pep talk about trying heroin? Because I don't actually want to do it," and she was all, "No, I just mean that if you *really* want heroin you find a way to do it," and I said, "Like I just don't want it enough? Are you judging me?" She definitely was but maybe not about heroin. I guess she was talking about the universal "you" who wants heroin.

I apologized for rambling and told her it was probably the tuberculosis talking, and she was very understanding, but when she tried to untie the rubbery tourniquet thingy from my arm it got stuck and she pulled too hard and punched herself right in the face. She sat on the floor in front of me and pinched her nose to try to stop the bleeding and then my doctor walked by the door and I held up my hands and said, "I DIDN'T DO IT," which—in retrospect—probably seemed even more suspicious.

Long story short, *oh my God, of course I have TB.* I collect diseases like other people collect Beanie Babies. I asked my doctor if we could call it "consumption" because TB sounds like that guy you lost your virginity to on a tractor in high school, and she said that was fine but I think she'd probably have agreed to anything I said because I WAS DYING OF CONSUMPTION.

Then she told me I was not dying, but I was pretty sure I was because consumption killed Doc Holliday and he was a damn doctor. She told me that Doc Holliday was a dentist, and while I don't like to be corrected I thought it was a good sign that she'd told me I was wrong, because usually when people are dying you just compassionately let them be stupid for their remaining time on earth.

Apparently TB is not all that uncommon and lots of people have it and never know they have it (much like buttworms) because there aren't usually symptoms unless you have an active infection. Luckily, my TB was inactive, so it was as lazy as I am. Apparently I'd been exposed to someone with active TB at some point and now I carry it around, along with all my deep-seated resentment of girls who were mean to me in junior high.

I wasn't contagious or sick. But having it in my immune-compromised body meant that I could become Typhoid Mary (or TB Jenny, in my case), and that made taking the RA injections that suppressed my immune system incredibly dangerous. The meds that I take to stop some of my diseases inhibit my immune system to the point where I wasn't allowed to take the injections keeping my rheumatoid arthritis at bay because it made me too susceptible to dying from TB, which I may have only gotten because the injections made my immune system so shitty that I couldn't fight it off. It's like a big game of "stop hitting yourself," except that you can't stop hitting yourself because your diseases and disorders work like falling dominoes and crash into each other in a way that makes you realize how delicate and impossible it can seem to stay human.

I feel like this is a depressing thought, and that's because it is depressing. In fact, when you're sick and can't move or are in pain for a long period of time, you often develop depression. And that makes it even harder to move or fight for yourself or see that you're worthy of the medication and treatment that seem almost impossible to get and will often save you while also killing you slowly. And then you gain weight because it hurts to move and then people tell you that it's your weight that is causing your problems and you want to stab them all in the thigh. And you get so many illnesses that you forget which ones you have and everyone on Facebook is like, "I bet you just have a gluten allergy," or "Have you tried prayer?" or "Have you been tested for [*fill in the blank with a million different things that will kill you*]?"

And frankly they're not wrong, because when this was going on a lot of people asked if I'd been tested for Hashimoto's disease, because it can cause depression and joint pain and a lot of the same problems I've struggled with forever. So when I went in for the blood work results I asked my doctor and she was like, "Yeah, of course you have Hashimoto's disease. You have a lot of diseases." And then she shrugged and went back to listing all the other things that were wrong with me, and that sort of sums up my whole life.

Luckily there is a drug that makes the TB in your body less likely to suddenly murder you, and if I took this very expensive medication for nine months I could safely go back on my injections that stop my RA symptoms. The TB medication made me sick and also fucked with my liver so much that I had to stop drinking alcohol for the whole nine months. After a few months of pausing the biologic injections my crippling RA started to show itself again and I was reminded how terrible it is to be untreated. I stuck with the voluntary nausea and expensive sobriety of TB treatment, which just goes to show you how bad RA really is and what I was willing to go through to get the injections again. Ironically, fighting off tuberculosis while having arthritis is when you want vodka the most, and nine months is a very long time. Usually if you go nine months without drinking you get a baby in the end, but all I got was less tuberculosis.

I did it though. And I was very proud of myself for the work it took. I felt really very healthy for the first time in a very long time, until right after that, when I discovered that I'd lost too much of my blood.

But I already covered that in another chapter, which is a relief because it sort of feels like we need a breather. And some blood, probably. And vodka.

Lots and lots of vodka.

The Secret to a Long Marriage

I get asked a lot about how I've managed to stay happily married for over two decades. The long answer is that we haven't always been happy. The short answer is that I was just too lazy to get divorced during the really hard parts. It seems fucked up that the long answer is shorter than the short answer, but in my defense, it was longer in my head but I didn't flesh it out properly. Mostly because I'm lazy.

At almost every reading, someone will tell me how much they love the conversations between Victor and myself that I share, and that they are still out there looking for their own Victor (or Jenny). This is occasionally followed by someone wearing a "TEAM VICTOR" shirt who stands up and loudly declares, "VICTOR IS A GODDAMN SAINT."

He totally is.

He's also a real asshole.

Those things aren't mutually exclusive, y'all. Honestly, it would suck if they were. If you were married to a saint you'd feel guilty all the time for fucking up like a regular human and eventually you'd assume that your spouse was possessed by a demon *because no one is perfect all the time*. The most rational explanation would be that this possessed motherfucker is just being perfect *at you* to mess with your head. Then you'd end up in jail for forcibly trying to exorcise someone because they were way too nice to not be a demonic entity. In fact, whenever I'm really mad at Victor I calm myself by looking at the positives, and sometimes I'm so mad the only positive I can come up with is, "At least he's not some sort of evil incubus pretending to be nice so that I let down my defenses long enough for him to steal my soul. Probably."

Usually, when people ask me about our great marriage I'm pleased (because it is hard work). But I am the first person to say that the secret to our incredible marriage is that the only stuff you know about is the stuff I've written down. Because frankly, the funny stuff is the most entertaining and what I want to share, but I am doing you a great disservice if you think that your relationship should always be wackiness and laughter and just enough frustration to be relatable and then wrapped up neatly at the end. Because that's only about 5 percent of our marriage. At least 50 percent is Victor yelling about empty cheese wrappers left on the floor and me lying about not leaving cheese wrappers on the floor, and then him yelling at me for lying about it and me pointing out that I'm not *technically* lying because *technically* I left those cheese wrappers on the kitchen counter and then Hunter S. Thomcat carried them away because he's a hoarder, and so *technically* the cat left them on the floor. A cat who obviously needs an intervention and does not need to see Mommy and Daddy fighting *because that's exactly the kind of trauma that just leads to more hoarding, Victor*. Then Victor disagrees. And that's his prerogative. But it gives me a nice alibi for later that afternoon when he finds all the empty pudding cups I've shoved under the couch.

Of course that only accounts for 55 percent of our relationship, and the other 45 percent is filled with boring-ass bullshit, banal silences, quiet lunches, and normal arguments about normal things. (I initially ended that sentence with "like how many otters are too many if you have a pool," but Victor says that isn't a "normal" thing, so instead I'll change it to "like how stingy Victor is with a pool we don't even use in the winter." Victor still thinks this is off. So fine. How about "like whether to add gutters to the roof"? Victor says he's fine with that one but I'd like to point out that we did get gutters and right now there is so much dirt and so many leaves in them that a tree is *literally* growing in the gutter. It's a small tree—like seven inches tall—but still . . . a tree. In. Our. Gutter. Now Victor just read this and is outside removing the evidence, and he's being pissy about it. "Why can't you clean the gutters?" And the answer is, "Gutters are scary as shit and that's why I didn't want them in the first place. You know who lives in gutters? Clown murderers. We bought tubes to catch clown murderers. GREAT CHOICE." Then Victor pointed out that the gutters that clown murderers hide in are sewer gutters, and it would be ridiculous to think that clown murderers could fit in our roof gutter, but right now there's a tree growing in ours so I think all bets are off. Plus, we've all learned that clown murderers are supernatural and can disappear at will and live inside sinks, so I'm pretty sure they can also make themselves tiny enough to hide in roof gutters. Then Victor argued that even my phrasing was questionable because "evil clown murderers" implied that they would be people who murder evil clowns and technically we'd *want* those around, and I get what he's saying from an organic pest control perspective but I still disagree because it's like when you buy a bunch of bats so that they eat all your mosquitoes and you're happy for that first day of no-mosquitoes but now you have a bat infestation in your house. Sometimes you have to think about the big picture. Victor agrees again but not about the same thing. But it's important to celebrate those times when you agree with each other so I count that as a win. Victor disagrees. Probably just out of spite.)

I got distracted there with mosquitoes and clown murderers and tiny trees but I had a point, and that point was that the secret to a long marriage is laziness. Basically one of you has to be too lazy to agree to a divorce.

When Victor and I first got married we struggled all the time. We were poor and almost lost our house. We argued a lot, which was a problem because I was under the impression that if you love someone you don't fight with them. My parents disagreed with each other and my mother mastered the quiet look of "*Jesus Christ, really?*" but they never fought in front of my sister and me, so I assumed that fighting was a sign that Victor and I shouldn't be together. In fact, after a few years I told my mother I thought we should get divorced. That's when she told me that she thought she'd done a disservice to me by hiding the fights she had with my dad because she'd thought that it would scare us. And probably it would have. But it also meant I never saw anyone model how to be mad and yell and talk it out and forgive. It's why I fight with Victor in front of our daughter. I fight in front of her because one day I want her to have a good marriage. (And because usually I'm right and it's nice to have a tiny Judge Judy in the back seat.) It's also why she will probably eventually say that fighting is not okay to do in front of kids and will hide all her fights, and each generation will continue to fuck up their children in their own special way. Sorry. I wish I had better advice here but I think what I've learned is that either way you probably fuck your kids up, but if you're just honest about it it's a great gift to give them because then they realize that you aren't perfect either and don't have all the answers and that it's okay to be messy sometimes. That's a hell of a gift for both of you, really.

After having that talk with my mom I decided to try harder. I tried not to judge us by any other standard than our own, because we were weird in our own crazy way and the only way forward was one we made ourselves.

That didn't mean it was easy. Our dynamic was so different from my parents'. I was entirely unprepared for living with Victor. I would have been fine dealing with Victor bringing a pet donkey to a bar or making moonshine in a homemade still in the backyard, but none of those things happened. My father hid live rattlesnakes in boxes because he was going to do something with them and then forgot until one of us opened them. But I knew how to deal with that because I'd seen the modeled behavior of my mother. Victor, on the other hand, spent the first year of our marriage squirreling away wads of cash in hidey-holes around the house. A bunch of twenties in a teacup. Three rolls of nickels in the bottom of a boot. Five bucks in a seashell. You might think it would be a welcome change to find unexpected cash rather than angry venomous animals, but the thing was that my dad had hidden the snakes from us so we wouldn't die as easily but Victor was hiding this money *from me*. Which was weird because we both worked full-time, we had a lot of bills, and I didn't spend money frivolously, so there was no reason for him to do it. But every time I found a wad of cash hidden in a beer cozy he'd swear he wouldn't do it again—and then promptly did it again. It was insane but eventually he admitted that he did it because he was afraid that one day we'd run out of money and he needed a safety net. One made of boot nickels, apparently.

I tried to understand him the same way he tried to understand me the night I got so mad at him I screamed uncontrollably and ran outside and hid in the bushes—until he found me and we realized I was standing in a fire ant bed. Instead of continuing the fight he used his seashell stash to buy some weird powder that stopped the pain. (The powder wasn't cocaine. I know it sounds like it was, but it wasn't.)

We were both crazy in ways that neither of us was prepared for, and it was hard as hell. It got easier as we learned how to pick our battles, but even now we'll have at least one fight a year where I think we'll get divorced. Victor will immediately quash the idea because he knows that no one else would put up with either of us and that I am entirely too lazy to fill out divorce paperwork. And he's too lazy to have to take care of two houses, because even if we got divorced I'd still be calling him every day to check my gutters for clown murderers and fix the Wi-Fi and turn the lights back on when I inevitably forgot to pay the bill or the pool otters chewed through the power lines. Laziness is what keeps us together through the hard days until the miracle that keeps us *wanting* to be together kicks in.

The miracle—it's a cliché, but clichés are clichés because they're true—is laughter. Because even when I'm at my most furious, Victor can say something to make me laugh and it all just washes away.

Last month we were traveling, and we don't really travel well together. I get irritated easily and I need lots of rest to not get sick, but Victor seemingly doesn't need food or sleep and thinks it's a waste of traveling if you're not constantly seeing every landmark ever invented. I was hungry and tired and I snapped at him for dragging me to another long line to see some historic church that looks like all the other churches, and he yelled at me for being a homebody who doesn't appreciate the world, and then I may have started crying, and then Victor looked at the man selling the tickets and said, "Is this where we kiss a wizard to remove a curse?"

It was so utterly random and Victor kept a straight face as the man just stared at him in confusion, and then I started giggling so hard I forgot how hungry I was. That is magic.

Victor once said that his favorite quote was Marilyn Monroe's: "If you can make a woman laugh you can make her do anything." It's true. Unless the thing you want her to do is put her cheese wrappers in the trash or stop touching the thermostat or not dress the cat up in baby clothes even though he looks amazing in them. Those are nonstarters. But you can make her forgive you. And love you. And forget about all the dumb shit you've done that she can't remember now but totally existed. And she can do the same.

And sometimes that's just enough.

So I'm Paying to Beat the Shit
Out of Myself?

"I bought this thing called a FasciaBlaster," my friend Maile told me, in one of those whispers that seem half an embarrassing confession and half like sharing the greatest secret in the world that you don't want anyone else to know.

It sounded like a video game but in fact it was a tool that she'd bought on the Internet that claimed to get rid of cellulite. "Does it work?" I asked, getting my credit card out.

"Well . . . I don't know yet. I'm in that stage where I look like a battered woman."

"Explain," I said. And she did.

She found a lady on Facebook who claimed to have a tool to eradicate cellulite, while at the same time claiming that cellulite does not actually exist. *This is a terrible business plan*, I thought to myself, but then I thought that maybe what the anti-cellulite lady was saying is that we should all just buy into the idea that cellulite isn't real. If someone says, "Ew, you have cellulite," we all look at them as if they've gone mad and gaslight the world into thinking that seeing cellulite is some sort of mass hallucination that is totally their problem and not ours. Then we can all wear bathing suits freely while making judgy assholes question their eyesight and sanity. I was all in. Unfortunately the real story isn't nearly so rational.

Instead, this woman had invented a sort of spiky plastic stick that you use to beat up the connective tissue in your body that holds your cellulite in place. It looks like a tiny coatrack for cats or a terrifying dildo. Her theory is that if you demolish all the connective tissue between your skin and your fat, then your cellulite won't show. I guess it's like if you squeeze a bunch of leopards against a chicken-wire fence, some of the leopard will squash through. The leopards are your fat and the chicken wire is your connective tissue and the parts of the leopards that squish through are your cellulite. If you get rid of the chicken wire, then you no longer have cellulite and now just have a bunch of angry, formerly squashed leopards who are uncaged and roaming free. It's possibly dangerous, but it looks sexy. Much like most cosmetic surgery, now that I think about it.

Maile explained that her thighs did *not* look sexy yet because she'd only been doing it for a few weeks and was covered in bruises "from ass to ankle."

"But that's how you know it's working," she said. "Giant bruises mean you're pummeling your fat hard enough." She mimed how she would take the tool, place it against her thigh, and tug it violently from side to side, much like a serial killer trying to use a hacksaw to dismember her own leg. Or like a lumberjack really angrily attacking a tree that had killed his mother, except that the tree was his own leg.

"So you paid eighty-nine dollars to beat the shit out of yourself?" I asked.

"I mean, basically," she said. "But just look at all these before-and-after pictures on Facebook."

I looked. They were impressive. But I wondered how many of them had also started working out and eating less after having to violently throttle their own fat each day. Still, the results were obvious, and I felt myself wondering if I should try it. "What's it called again? Kill Yourself Slowly? How to Get a Blood Clot in Thirty Days? Deep Vein Thrombosis and Skinny Thighs?" She laughed with me because she's not insane, or is insane in the same way as most women who think their imperfections should be violently physically assaulted.

My anxiety popped up and screamed slightly louder than my need to have smoother fat. "But what if my fascia is like Samson's hair and it's the only thing keeping me strong? I mean, it's strong enough to hold up my fat even when it's being beaten to death. I'm already weak enough without getting rid of all of my supporting cast."

Maile shrugged. "Seems unlikely."

"What if I try this and my connective tissue was the only thing keeping all my fat in place and then all my leg fat falls into my feet and I have to buy new shoes and start ripping out all my pubic hair?"

Maile stared at me, probably because she'd never considered the possibility of having fat feet the size of inflatable rafts. "Not sure I'm following."

"I've never had to get a bikini wax," I explained, "because my inner-thigh fat hides any stray lady garden foliage. But if all my fat falls out, then my accidental hairnet disappears."

"That is a very good point. You're saving a fortune in waxing costs alone."

"Or what if one of the bruises becomes a blood clot and then an embolism and then I get a stroke and half of my body is paralyzed and then Victor gets arrested for domestic abuse because I'm covered in internal bleeds that no one believes I gave myself from beating up my cellulite with a pointy stick I bought on the Internet?"

"Well, you'd look good in the hospital, probably?" she offered. "Honestly, I never really thought about that. This is feeling stupider now."

"But I think I'm still in? If I'm only halfway through with the process when I get a stroke and don't have the ability to domestically abuse my fat, will you come do it for me?"

"*Of course I will*," she said, patting my hand. "That's what's friends are for. I will beat *the shit* out of your fat."

I'd like to say that this ended with both of us laughing and vowing to use the FasciaBlaster only to hit stupid people with, but in truth I wrote down the name and wondered if I could charge it on my business account if I wrote about it.

Maile tried to blame the fat blaster on the insanity that comes when you're in the middle of a divorce, as she was, but we've both done way stupider things in the name of beauty over the years, so that seemed unlikely. Just a few years ago we'd gone together to try a weight loss experiment that consisted of us stripping down to our underwear, having insultingly thin strangers slather hot mud onto our bodies, and then being wrapped up mummylike in plastic cling wrap in a heated room, like terrible leftovers no one would ever want. (I felt like too much sausage being stuffed in a casing. Then I started craving sausage. It was a vicious circle.) The sweating and the mud were supposed to make you shrink but an hour later I found that I had *gained* three inches. Maile helpfully suggested that I was probably allergic to mud and was swollen from a reaction, but I'm pretty sure my pores just got hungry and sucked up all of the mud like it was an all-you-can-eat smoothie.

Besides that, Maile's divorce was so amicable that she and her husband were still having family dinners and planning vacations together. They hadn't announced it to the world at large though because it seemed exhausting to try to have to tell people that they really were still great friends but just great friends who weren't going to live together anymore.

"There should be divorce reveals," I said. "Like when people reveal that they're pregnant and they make a crazy video or they reveal the genitals of the baby by cutting into a cake that's either penis or vagina."

(Clarification: The penis cake is blue. The vagina cake is pink. It's not a cake *made* of penises and vaginas. It's made of food coloring and far too much trust in your cake decorator. Once I picked up Hailey's fifth-birthday cake and for some reason it said "HAPPY GRADUATION" on it. I told her it was because she'd graduated to the next year and she was fine, but what if the decorator fucks up your genital cake? What if the cake is yellow? What does that mean? We're going to buy a dog? We ran out of food coloring? We stopped placing gender stereotypes on babies based on baked goods?)

"Oh my God, we should do a reveal for your divorce," I said.

"How about a picture of me lying in bed and there's a cartoon bubble of me saying, 'FINALLY IT'S ALL MINE,' while I roll around back and forth? And also the bed is full of pots of macaroni and cheese that I'm eating straight out of."

"Oh my God," I said. My eyes teared up a little. "That's what heaven looks like."

"And then I lean over and snort a line of powdered macaroni cheese off the bedside table."

"Jesus Christ. Now *I* want a divorce."

She nodded knowingly. "It's pretty awesome sometimes," she admitted.

But then I didn't get a divorce *or* the fat blaster because I'm too lazy for either one and also because ripping your fat out seems a lot like accidental exercise and there's no way I'm falling for that. But Maile and I decided to be friends forever and to go eat some macaroni and cheese and laugh until it hurt. It was amazing.

Wouldn't it be great if the chapter ended right there? So uplifting and brave and accidentally inspirational? Answer: only if you use the word "brave" *incredibly* loosely. But it feels dishonest to leave it there because I have to apply my personal motto of "WAIT, I CAN MAKE IT WORSE."

And I can because today I got a bunch of my face burned off with vagina lasers.

What are vagina lasers? you're probably asking yourself as you slowly back away. *Are they lasers you install in your vagina? What is even happening here?*

I'm glad you asked that, because yesterday I was at the doctor's getting blood work but they put me in the waiting room with the gyno table and I was surrounded by *WAY* too many posters yelling at me about how much I needed vagina lasers and I felt very judged because YOU DON'T KNOW MY LIFE, VAGINA LASERS, AND I DON'T APPRECIATE WHATEVER IT IS YOU'RE IMPLYING. But then my doctor came in and I was like, "What are vagina lasers? Are they lasers you install in your vagina?" and she was like, "I'm fine. Thanks for asking. How are you?" and point taken, but in my defense she left me in an empty room for twenty minutes where I'd been fighting with aggressive vagina laser propaganda, so technically this was her fault and totally went against her oath of "First, do no harm."

She explained that the lasers were used to laser the inside of your vagina and I was like, "Ew, no. Stop talking," and she said, "Did you think you could get them installed in a vagina? That's better? Like some sort of genital laser pointer?" and I explained that I was thinking less of a cat toy/presentation tool and more of a defense system for when you really want to make it clear that "no means no, asshole," and she just stared at me so I clarified by making small "Pew! Pew!" laser-gun noises, and then she shook her head and was like, "No. We don't offer that. *No one offers that.*"

And then I explained that was probably for the best because I can't even figure out how to set the clock on the microwave, so I'd always be losing the remote to my vagina and be shooting cats and burning holes in my shoes, but I pointed out that it *would* be kind of cool to have a light saber inside your vagina and then I instantly regretted my phrasing.

Long story short, my doctor said she could not install lasers in my vagina but that since I was there we should go ahead and laser off "that thing" on my nose because apparently the same lasers they use inside your cootch are great for zapping away age spots and blemishes. I agreed to let her laser me, although it was a bit disconcerting that she's a doctor and referred to a part of my body as "that thing." I don't know the medical term for it either, though. It's just a weird lump that's been there for years. The thing on my nose, I mean. Not my vagina. Although my vagina has been around for ages as well. NOT THAT MY VAGINA HAS "BEEN AROUND." Jesus. I'm going to stop this paragraph now.

She zapped about ten spots on my face and it smelled like

something was burning, and turns out that something was me. And over the next few weeks the spots turned black and I went from being slightly sensitive about my age spots to having them so dark it honestly looked like I'd had a series of constellations tattooed directly onto my face. I waited for the spots to scar over and then flake away, because if you pick at them you get a permanent scar, and I considered that maybe this was some sort of psychological punishment designed to make you so self-conscious that when they finally faded you were just happy for the original imperfections that weren't now black, flaky messes. I suddenly found myself grateful that this sort of mess wasn't also happening inside my vagina and counted myself lucky.

A week later the spots had all healed and underneath was lovely unmarked skin with no bumps or dark spots.

And about eight weeks later all the spots had returned, along with "that thing" on my nose. Because of course they did.

But it's fine because I've realized that the imperfections in my face, body, and brain—and vagina—are what make me the unique person I am. They tell a story. And my vagina's story would be its screaming, "I SAW WHAT HAPPENED TO YOUR FACE. KEEP THOSE LASERS AWAY FROM ME." And that's a little ridiculous because I'm not nearly flexible enough for my vagina to see my nose and also because we all know that next month I'm going to hear about some ridiculous blood ritual or human sacrifice that makes your tits firmer and be all over it. Yes, I realize this is a flaw I have, but in the end isn't self-acceptance what this is all about?

Yes. It is.*****

———————————

***** That and butt plumping by injecting the blood of ancient virgin saints, eighteen sessions of which I have scheduled next month.

Anxiety Is a Lost Watch I Never Saw

Sometimes I become paralyzed. Out of fear mostly. Fear of doing the wrong thing. Fear of making the wrong choices. Fear of confrontation. Fear of not being kind or right or helpful. I think most "normal" people deal with this in small ways, but my fear is different. It can incapacitate me. At best figuratively, and at worst literally. My hands curl up into fists. My frame cramps itself into small, painful fetal shapes, as if somehow my body wants to be less of itself—to disappear completely. And when it gets too overwhelming I tell myself the story my grandmother told me when I was young . . . the story of the watch that almost made me not be.

That sounds like a sentence fragment but it's not. Or rather, it is, but it's still true. Things can be wrong and true at the same time.

When my grandmother was young a boy liked her and wanted to marry her. But she didn't love him back, so she was friendly but noncommittal. One day at school he gave her his watch to borrow but that night after working on the farm she saw that it was missing.

She was sure that she'd have to marry him after that, because how else do you make up for losing an expensive watch you could never replace? She and her family searched for hours through the farm and finally her brother found it in the plowed field that surrounded their house. She was so relieved she cried, and she immediately gave the watch back. I'm not sure what happened to that boy or to that watch but it's strange to think that I might never have been born if my grandmother had married a man because she felt bad about a watch. In fact, as I write this, it seems insane that anyone would agree to marry someone because they felt bad about losing something so silly. But at the time it seemed unquestionable . . . for her and for me. Out of a sense of duty, of fear, of doing what she thought was right, she could have changed her whole world. And his. And mine. And yours, because right now you'd be reading another book altogether.

I used to think she told me that story to teach me not to borrow things I couldn't replace, but now I wonder if she wasn't teaching me something more. That sometimes you have to do the hard thing. Sometimes you have to say no. Sometimes you have to make waves. Because otherwise you can get swept away. This is a lesson I am still learning.

Sometimes my anxiety gets hard in ways that you might not expect. If you struggle with anxiety you probably know this feeling . . . the paralysis. Supposedly when you're scared you have a fight-or-flight response. You either stab the shit out of whatever scares you or you run from it. I don't do either, though, partly because I can never find the knives and hate physical exercise, but more because before I get to fight-or-flight I get stuck. Literally. I can't move. I can't speak or write. I worry about every little thing. I worry about the silence I'm stuck in. I worry that the silence speaks louder than the person I am. And then I get more stuck. And suddenly it's been days since I replied to people on the Internet and the pressure gets worse and I panic that people I haven't responded to are mad at me so I ignore their emails and I don't look at my DMs or my texts and I don't answer my phone or listen to voicemails because if I just wait until my mind gets better maybe I can deal with this then. But I don't. Because it doesn't. And instead I look at these unopened emails from friends and family and colleagues until I have memorized the subject lines by heart and think about how strange it is that they probably think that I'm ignoring them when in fact I am utterly haunted by them.

But why? They would probably understand if I told them the problem. In fact, because I collect broken people like myself, they'd probably be relieved to find that they aren't alone (although they'd probably hate that the ball was back in their court and now they had to respond to me). And those who didn't understand wouldn't toil over it and tear their hair out like I do. They'd read my "I'M TOO CRAZY FOR EMAIL" email and think, *Huh, what a weirdo*, and then never think about it again. I don't know what it's like not to have anxiety but I assume it's like that. It's probably not exhausting. It probably doesn't end with eighty-seven rewritten and unsent emails and a to-do list that never ends and chapters written and deleted so many times that you forget what it is you've said and you just want to set fire to your brain to clear away all the brush and start over.

It's a strange thing . . . to be tangled up in things no one else really cares about. To be so busy with worry that your constant back-and-forth looks like utter inaction. To be so afraid of doing something wrong that you end up doing something worse. To be exhausted by a marathon that looks like complete paralysis on the outside but feels like being on both sides of a violent tug-of-war on the inside.

It's not just emails and chapters and voicemails. It's more.

It's the whole world. It's every terrible thing that happens in the universe that I feel like I need to speak out about but then don't because fear stops me. Then I fear that inaction. I fear that my silence is equal to agreement with terrible things. I fear when I do speak out that I've done so inelegantly, or wrongly, or that I've made things worse. That it's not my place to speak or that it's not my place to be silent.

I read and read and read and know every detail of the terrible thing, waiting to find that one detail that will make me know for certain what to say or how to act. But it never comes. And that makes sense, because if simple words fixed terrible things, then terrible things would not exist. So I speak.

Sometimes.

And sometimes I fail. And sometimes I flourish. And sometimes I change my mind halfway through. And sometimes I write long and emotional things to help myself understand an issue and then never share them. Sometimes I speak only to myself. And that's okay.

But sometimes I am loud. Sometimes the voices in my head are so angry I have to let them go. Sometimes I can do nothing else but speak my mind and do the things that must be done, because the pain of not doing them is greater than the pain of doing them. And it is wonderful and terrible all at once.

And sometimes it is small and sometimes it is big, but always it is hard.

And always it is worth it.

And when I struggle with the little things that seem so small and unimportant, I remind myself that it's okay to struggle and to allow myself to find my own speed. Small things can be important. Words, decisions, pauses, compassion, lost watches, short stories . . . there are whole worlds in these small things. And I live in these worlds. And (sometimes) I'm glad I do.

I remember the lost watch, that little bit of nothing that almost changed everything, and I remind myself of what I think my grand-mother was telling me with her story. That all small terrors pass. That fear can make you think irrational thoughts. That you are only ever truly trapped when you give up and allow yourself to be.

Don't give up.

The Eight Billionth Argument
I Had with Victor This Week

Me: My electric toothbrush is broken so I need a new one.

Victor: Just because the battery is out it doesn't mean your toothbrush is broken. It still works.

Me: No. Because the battery is out.

Victor: Yes, but it still works as a toothbrush. You just have to brush with your hands.

Me: Like some sort of animal?

Victor: No. Because animals don't have thumbs. Or brush their teeth.

Me: I brush animals' teeth. The cat's toothbrush still works. You want me to use the cat's toothbrush? Is that what you're suggesting? Because that's how you get cholera.

Victor: That's not how you get cholera.

Me: Fine. Feline leukemia. *Way to scare the cats, dude.*

Victor: That's not . . . AAAAH. YOU CAN STILL USE YOUR

TOOTHBRUSH EVEN IF IT DOESN'T VIBRATE. IT'S NOT BROKEN.

Me: I didn't say my toothbrush was broken. I said my *electric* toothbrush was broken. Because now it's just a toothbrush. Like when escalators are broken they are still broken escalators. If you called to say that your escalator was broken the escalator repair people wouldn't say, "It's not broken. They're stairs now."

Victor: Please stop talking.

Me: It's like saying that your toothbrush is broken if you found out I used it on the dog because I didn't know if cats and dogs could share a toothbrush. It still works but you'd probably say it was unusable now.

Victor: *Did you brush the dog's teeth with my toothbrush?*

Me: No. Because you'd get all overreacty. Plus, she got scared by the vibraty noises. OH MY GOD she can use my broken toothbrush! Wait. Is that okay?

Victor: *NONE OF THIS IS OKAY.* HOW CLOSE DID YOU GET TO THE DOG WITH MY TOOTHBRUSH?

Me: Not close enough to do any good. She was freaked. Like, I'm considering getting a vibrator just to wave at her when she chews on my shoes. But it seems weird to show people that your dog is afraid of a vibrator because *what is that all about*?

Victor: Why don't you go buy a new toothbrush?

Me: We are totally of one mind.

Victor: God forbid.

Sometimes There Is Beauty in Breaking

I draw when I can't write.

I draw when I hurt.

I draw more than I would like to admit.

I was just drawing myself. The me of now, when I'm broken more than usual. The me I drew was a shadow because right now I'm in that bad part of depression. That step past sad. The step into numb. It's not a good numb. It's uncomfortable and out of control and I wonder if I'm even real.

My face doesn't fit right—like a mask that's slipped. I could drink to numb the pain of being numb but it's not a long-term solution and I'm too tired for it. Does that even make sense? Numbing the pain of numbness? It does if you've been here before.

I am hollow. Scooped out. Empty. I am a shadow. I write this on my drawing and I know that it will change my art from something people can relate to and see themselves in to something that people may fear. Something "othering" that makes normal people hesitantly back away, or hesitantly step closer—but both are in bad ways. I would soothe them and tell them I'll be okay, but it's easier to pretend to be fine and hide the brokenness. To paint a false smile and fake that my body is fully mine until it is again.

I look back at the drawing. The shadow of a girl running into the night, but the night is not dark. The edges are. The parts around the edges of the world that get black and loose and are invisible to normal people. People whose eyes have adjusted to this kind of darkness can see in the night, so the stars in my picture are as bright as the night surrounding them. The edges are dark, and I know that a *real* artist would look at this and say that the perspective is all wrong. You can't throw shadows in the night. Darkness can't be deeper than the night. It's all wrong. And it is. But it is my perspective; it's as wrong as I am.

The dog barks to go out and I take her out into the night for a walk. It's late and everyone else is asleep. I blend into the night. It swallows me like a cloak. I always told Hailey that being afraid of the dark was silly because the thing about darkness is that it's not just a place for things to hide. It's a cloak that hides you as well. The night can be a friend. And that's a good thing to know, but only when your head is working properly and you can assure yourself that once you step back into the house you'll cast a shadow again instead of being one. That promise doesn't exist tonight and I hurry back inside, feeling claustrophobic in the darkness that seems as if it will consume or wash away what little bit of me I have left.

I unhook the dog from her leash, thinking about how to finish the drawing . . . going over the words in my head. *"Hollow," "empty," "missing."* I am running to find myself, and I don't know where I will be or when I will find me. I don't know if I will find the old me or a new one. I don't know how I feel about either of these things. I don't remember how to feel like I did before. I know it will pass. I remind myself it will pass. It's like reminding myself that I don't need to breathe when I'm underwater. My body doesn't believe it. My head doesn't either. But my past says it will pass. And my past has never lied the way depression lies to me, so I take a deep breath and keep moving forward, even though I've forgotten where I was going.

The dog rushes off, chasing the cat, who runs into my legs as I'm walking. I gasp and try to calm him but he scurries, panicked, across the counter to avoid the dog and my feet and he skitters sideways, his catlike balance momentarily deserting him as he flees, terrified, knocking over my large stone dove on the table.

At least, I thought she was stone. She's not. She's lived on my table with her male companion for so many years I don't even remember where they came from anymore. I can't remember them ever not gracing the table together. But now she is smashed open on the kitchen tile. She is broken from her base, and dozens of pieces have flown across the room and scattered across the floor.

She is hollow. Except for the pedestal, which is filled with something strange, probably to keep her upright . . . a white sort of spun glass or excelsior. I pick her up with shaky hands, hoping her body is at least in one piece so I can salvage part of her. I hear my daughter's bedroom door open upstairs.

"*Mom?*" she calls down nervously in case I'm a burglar or something that goes bump in the night. "*What was that?*"

"Nothing," I assure her from the kitchen. "The cat just knocked something over. Go back to bed, honey," I say with what I think is maybe what my voice sounds like when I'm not having to pretend to be whole.

The dove is broken. Her beak is gone and I can't find all the pieces I need to make her whole again. I crawl on the floor to pick up the pieces I can find. I never find them all but I try. I have to keep my family safe from the jagged, broken parts that might be left behind. I notice there is blood on my foot but I don't know if it's from the cat scratching me or from the dove. It doesn't matter anyway. What's done is done. But I still grieve for the bird. The broken pieces softly clink together, cradled in my skirt. The matched set will no longer match. The male dove will now forever stand guard alone.

But it's not fair, I think. And I look at the pieces I've picked up and see the alabaster inside that was hidden, and the hollowness, and the strange, beautifully ugly excelsior—the mystery that made her stand so long, and the mystery that made her fall so hard.

I won't let it end like this. I decide that if she has to be broken I will make her breaking into art, to honor her and keep her. I take my camera and capture her. The broken pieces and the whole ones.

She is broken but the round top of the pedestal she stood on takes on the appearance of a cracked emu egg. It reminds me of the hollowed-out Styrofoam eggs my mother would fill with miniature spring scenes at Easter when I was little, and I realize I haven't thought of those magical things since I was small. The excelsior shines. There is beauty in the brokenness, and even though I'd rather have her whole and perfect again, I can still recognize that she's turned into something else in her breaking. She is art. At least to some eyes. Trash to others. It's all in the seeing, after all.

If you look close you can tell she's special. She has a story to tell. Broken things always do. I keep her on my counter, turned toward the window. You can't immediately tell that she's broken, but she is.

She is hollow. She is shattered. She is scooped out, but at least for tonight I have filled her back up, with meaning and symbolism and strength. She becomes a small talisman. With the right set of eyes you can see her magic.

I remind myself that my eyes are working differently than most people's right now. Being in the dark too long will do that to you. And sometimes there's a small blessing in that.

I turn back to my drawing. I see myself—the self that I've drawn. I see my shadow. I see all the colors that make it up. I am reminded that (although it's hard for our eyes to see) black is made of *all* of the colors, not an absence of them. I tell myself I will be me again soon. But until I am, I may be a broken dove, reminding others of the terrible but fantastic visions that come with an unquiet mind and the strange burden of sometimes becoming a shadow.

I finish my drawing.

I decide to keep the broken dove even though I can already hear Victor in my head telling me that she's too broken to save. I will nod and agree but I still won't part with her. She will tell a story to people who will wonder what magic she must have if she's still treasured even in this state.

She is shattered but she is special.

And if you don't look too closely you can hardly tell she's broken.

A Note: The next morning Victor did see the broken bird, and when I explained why I couldn't throw her away he told me I should make kintsugi *with her.* Kintsugi *is the Japanese art of fixing broken things with lacquer dusted with powdered gold to treat repair as part of the history, rather than disguising the breakage. The brokenness becomes part of the story and the beauty of the piece. And it made me smile a little, but I explained that I couldn't find all the pieces. He shrugged and said, "They're here. They can't just disappear. We'll find them eventually." And then he headed to his office. Sometimes things surprise you. Sometimes they're more than just meets the eye.*

No One Wants Your Handwritten "Good for One Free Massage" Coupons, Darryl

I was standing in line at the grocery store thinking about how much I hate grocery stores and skimming through one of those ladies' magazines that make you feel bad about yourself, and it said that the secret to a healthy relationship can be found in four things: romantic rose petals on the bed, honesty, sensual massage, and a series of sex positions that I'm pretty sure would result in hurt feelings and probably a torn rotator cuff. I've been in a moderately healthy relationship for decades and the thing I've learned is that most of this is bullshit. But I thought I'd explore it a little more (other than the sex positions—because my parents are going to read this and also I'm good enough at sex that I don't have to risk dislocation to keep things exciting).

So let's check these out realistically, shall we?

ROSE PETALS

I'm not sure what's so sexy about decapitating roses, especially since they're super expensive and I'm basically paying to mangle them (and myself with the thorns). The rose petals dry up almost immediately, so basically it's like you have crunchy dead leaves in your bed, sticking to everything and embedding themselves in your butt crack. Basically you just intentionally brought in the whole reason why people don't have sex outside on the ground and also now your fingers are bleeding.

HONESTY

Honesty is nice in small amounts but it's very easy to confuse "truth" with "just being a dick." And while I appreciate not being lied to, I appreciate even more not having someone tell me that I cut my hair too short again WHEN I DIDN'T EVEN ASK YOU.

SENSUAL MASSAGE

No. Just. No.

I realize that that some people really love to give sensual massages but it's been my experience that the people who are the least adept at massages are the most likely to give you a handwritten coupon book for rubdowns. It's always either so soft that you feel like you're being tickled in the worst possible way, or it's so extreme that you suspect you're being punished. You're not massaging me. You're just pushing me. But slightly less aggressively than an actual assault. So you're failing at romancing me *and* at assaulting me.

Here is a firsthand, realistic exploration of sensual massage:

1. Tell your partner what you like and don't like, because communication is key. "Don't touch me there. Or there. Nope. Okay, I feel fat now. You know what? You can touch my ankles and the skin on the back of my hands."

2. No one has the same erogenous zones. You might think a rigorous Swedish squishing of the scrotal sack would be wanted, but I've found it almost always brings screams. Are they screams of pleasure? I thought so until I heard the pop. Maybe I should have used more Pam. (Pro tip: If you don't have massage oil you can use cooking oil. If you don't have cooking oil you can use nonstick cooking spray. ["Can," not "should."]) Also, it's very seductive to tell your man you're bringing Pam into your bedroom. Sure, it's really an expired petroleum-based spray that has gone rancid, but it's a nice teaser until they figure it out. This light dishonesty is called "foreplay" and it gets funnier every time. Your partner might disagree but trust me . . . it's coming back around. Comedy is all about timing.

3. Some people say that the music you listen to sets the mood and this is why I invest in a good Norwegian death metal album. First of all, the deadly fast headbanging pace helps you remember that the faster and more violently you rub, the better. Ever try to go below the speed limit in a sports car? No. Same thing with erotic massages. Pummel that scrotum. Really throttle it until he's singing along with those full-throated Viking screams. Also, the fact that neither of you speak Norwegian means you can imagine the words mean anything. Maybe the singer is screaming about sensual massages and how he likes candlelight and kittens. Maybe he's saying that those jeans you bought last week that you're still questioning look super good on you. Maybe he's yelling at your husband for not taking the garbage out. *Again.* Even though it's his fault that the trash is full because *who cleans out*

the fridge and doesn't empty the trash? That's like cleaning up by putting the dirty clothes in the kitchen sink
rather than the hamper. You're just making the problem
more visible. *What is wrong with you? What are you even
thinking?!* That's what the Norwegian guy is saying, I
mean. Not me. I'm fine with it. I'm totally understanding
and I love you. Relax.

4. Use your words. Words give way to emotion and emotion
    increases the intensity of the massage. Romantic tension
    is a playful thing, much like loving titty-twisters or molten
    candle wax unexpectedly dripped on sensitive skin. Try
    whispering something like "Did you turn in our taxes? Are
    you sure? What if they got lost at the post office? Because
    if you made a mistake we're both going to jail." You can tell
    it's working if they start to tense up with pleasure. Don't
    stop now. Keep whispering in their ear. "It's just that I
    thought I saw the tax papers you were supposed to mail in
    the trash earlier. You didn't accidentally throw them out
    during some sort of blackout-drunk moment, did you? I'm
    only asking because you emptied the fridge and didn't take
    out the garbage and so I'm wondering if you're drunk or
    high on meth. I ask because I care. You're too pretty for
    jail, darling."

5. Everyone has to fart, and that's the only thing either
    of you can think about. And now it's worse because
    you're at a weird angle and you're pushing on some-
    one or someone is pushing on you. All you can think is,
    *Should I just fart? Will it be like a compliment, showing
    how relaxed I am? Will my partner be able to smell it*

over the scent of the cabbagey fridge garbage defrosting in the trash in the next room? Can I blame it on the dog even though the dog isn't in here? Would it be weird if I stopped to bring in the dog for an erotic massage?

6. *The dog won't stop looking at me. It's super creeping me out. This isn't worth the fart freedom.*

7. Throw the dog out, because turns out dogs love Pam. Clean any bites well. Irrigate wounds. Consider a tetanus shot. How long has it been since you got one? What happens if you get too many? Spend twenty minutes on WebMD looking at tetanus info. Ten minutes later realize that you probably have bubonic plague.

8. Let your partner know you have bubonic plague. Because that's the responsible thing to do. Listen to him unsupportively yell at you because apparently *he's the one with all the dog bites and he told you not to use the Pam in the first place and why did the dog even need to come in?* Feel upset but then realize it's the pain and fear talking. The pain and fear of losing you to the bubonic plague. Which you definitely have.

9. Snuggle up together with bandages after you pick up the antibiotics needed to stave off the bacteria of the dog bites while you reflect on your life before you got the plague. It was a good life. You were loved. You have rose petals in your crevices. Be proud. This is what love is all about.

This is the moment where most people are nodding in agreement and pointing out that this is exactly why people pay lots of money

Jenny Lawson

for professional massages, and I am with you, and then you say, "You should try a couple's massage!" and then I sigh and start a new list:

1. Take a romantic vacation to recover from the trauma of the massage. Sign up for a couple's massage at the hotel. If you're new to this concept (like I was) it's when you and your partner get a massage at the same time in the same room. Why? *No goddamn idea,* but every hotel will guilt you into one and it will cost more than your first car.

2. Take off all your clothes. Now let a stranger squoosh you. Try to distract yourself from the awkwardness by looking at your husband, who is being slathered in oil by a stranger. Remind yourself that you can't punch the woman rubbing on your naked husband in the face, and in fact you will be required to tip her. Do not relax, because then you're going to fart in front of your husband *and* two strangers.

3. Become keenly aware of the sound of an air mattress leaking and then realize it's the hissing noise your husband makes when the masseuse presses down hard on his back. Try not to laugh. Laugh even harder. When your partner gets mad because you're laughing through the most expensive massage of your life, explain that you can't relax when it sounds like there's a bunch of angry snakes in the room.

4. Pick a skin scrub that will rip your skin off. I chose coffee grounds, so basically I paid to have expensive garbage rubbed into me by strangers while my husband involuntarily threatened me in Parseltongue.

5. Consider separate vacations. Have a fight. Be mad that you're wasting time fighting on your vacation. Realize that everyone else in the resort is also fighting or is about to

fight or just got through fighting. Decide to skip to the part where everything is cool again because you've been married long enough to know how to forgive each other.

6. Order room service. Binge-watch *Battlestar Galactica* on your laptop. Together. Scratch his back in that place that he can never reach. Make those inside jokes that only you two find funny. Discover that the things that work for your relationship may not be candles and blindfolds and poetry. Realize that that's what love is all about after all and be forever thankful you finally have the kind of relationship that allows you to be honest about how terribly overrated sensual massage is for you.

So, I guess honesty *is* an important cornerstone in a successful relationship now that I think about it.

Touché, ladies' magazine. *Touché indeed.*

I Feel It in My Bones

I feel it in my bones.

The rain that hasn't come.

It doesn't make sense but it's true. I wake up at two a.m. and my hands ache and throb. I can feel my pulse in my feet. My wedding ring is too tight and I slide my fingers under my pillow to unclench my fists.

It's going to rain, I say. Like a strange atmosphere building up inside me. A storm of tiny fractures inside my bones. My husband makes a half-awake noise of sympathy.

I used to think it was all in my head. An old wives' tale about arthritis. *You can't predict the weather with bones*, I'd say. But my skeleton says other things.

I take two aspirin and get back into bed. My head is too full of clouds. My face burns and my hands hold a fever that cracks like firewood.

It's going to rain, I say to my hands and to my feet. *It's going to rain and then this will pass.* An hour goes by and the pain moves to my legs. I want to run and stretch the pain away. I want to wrap my fragile bones in soft white tissue, like they're delicate china cups. I want my mother to stroke my hair and say, *It's just growing pains*, like she did those years when I grew too quickly.

Then I hear it. The muffled, uneven tapping. The slow but insistent beating on the metal roof. The gentle pinging noise of the early-morning rain cooling the warm metal.

I reach out to press my hand to the window glass. It's cold, and the coolness is a relief on my hands.

It's raining. I sigh. It's a relief in more ways than you can imagine. My swollen parts will return to normal soon. The dam has broken. The worry of feeling insane passes a little. Not entirely, though. Because who can hold rain in their bones? Rain that hasn't even come? I know who. The same person who holds fog in her head. Who is undone by the pull of full moons. Who is far too sensitive to the strange whims of a body and mind that listen too much to the world.

In some ways it's a relief to feel the pain of coming rains. It assures me that the storms in my head are real too. And that they will, as well, pass in time. I wonder if there's a weather pattern for depression. A barometric pressure for anxiety. A bad wind for sleeplessness and fear. I wonder why I'm so much rain in bones and fog in thought. I wonder why distant hurricanes scream inside me and why sometimes the air grows thick and too heavy, leaving me a stranded sailing ship on a too-still sea for as long as the depression settles.

I move my other hand to the window. The heat of my hand creates an aura that surrounds it, as if I can finally see the invisible parts of me that stretch beyond the boundary of my skin. *It's raining*, I whisper.

How do you do that? Victor asks sleepily. *How do you always know?*

It's easy, I say. Although "easy" is not the right word.

I feel it in my bones.

Editing Is Hell. Mostly for Editors.

Let's talk a little about the process of editing a book.

DON'T STOP READING. Yes, I know editing sounds boring, but it's not. It's awful and painful and hilarious and mortifying but not boring. I have a small, permanent lump on my forehead from pounding it on my desk during the editing of my books. The whole process was so ridiculous (mainly because I was involved in something too grown-up to be trusted with) that I started to take notes about it so I could look back on it if I started to believe the hype that I am in any way qualified to be an intelligent writer.

So . . . editing. First off, there are a ton of different editors who help fix shit. My main editor, the copy editors, the production editor, the legal editors, my group of four friends who read drafts and tell me what doesn't make sense, the squirrels who live in my computer and phone who run spellcheck and who autocorrect texts like "I'll just be here in the bar, marinating" to "I'll just be here in the bar, masturbating."

I didn't actually notice that autocorrect until the next day. It was a group text. No one corrected me. Or shook my hand.

Sorry. Got off track. I blame my editor, or lack thereof, since I'm doing this all with only my ADD meds and the "help" of the squirrels.

I'm a big fan of self-editing because I tend to overwrite, so I have thousands of pages of writing that will never see the light of day, and even when I have something I like I usually try to delete half of it before I submit it to anyone. This makes my writing more succinct, and I know you wouldn't think that from the chapters that appear to be nothing but a dangerous run-on sentence, but I assure you, it's much worse before I cut the extra-crazy stuff out.

I used to think that was what editors did, and in fact, when I was still working on my first book a very successful editor was interested in it and I was like, "No thanks. I know how punctuation works," which was a total lie and also shows how incredibly stupid I was, because I had no idea that your editor is the person who buys your book for the publishing house and helps you finish it. I thought they were someone you pay to fix your shit. Learn from my mistakes.

Luckily, I later found a great agent, Neeti Madan, and she helped me find the perfect editor, Amy Einhorn, and both of them helped make my books what they would become. This involves months and months of drafts of the book going back and forth with notes written in margins from every sort of editor until you think the book is perfect. Then the book comes out and you immediately see a mistake you didn't catch and that's how you know it's yours.

During the editing process I lost track of which editor was noting that there should be changes, but the changes were such a confusing ball of weirdness that I kept notes on the details, because some of the editing suggestions were often more entertaining than the story.

Some people will read this chapter and feel very bad for my editors, and that is fair, and you should send them cookies and vodka, but on the other hand, it's people like me who ensure they will always have jobs and also provide great stories to tell their friends at bars. Where they are (probably) not masturbating, *thank you very much, autocorrect.*

ACTUAL NOTES I PUT IN THE UNEDITED MANU-SCRIPTS THAT EDITORS HAD TO DEAL WITH:

- "Words should go here. I haven't figured them out but basically just a variation of twenty-seven letters I haven't decided how to organize yet."
- "I wrote something awesome here and then the cat unplugged my computer. It was so, so good though. Can we just put something here that says, '*You would have loved this*'?"
- "Can I insert a video of a happy baby goat here? Because people love that shit. I never see that in ebooks or in paperbacks so it would be pretty revolutionary. We should start that."
- "This is the part where I would easily segue into my point using a very witty and subtle jumble of words that I simply can't think of right now *because amaretto is delicious*."

When I was working on my first book one of the editors sent me a cheat sheet for the shorthand used in fixing shit and she told me to not be afraid to "stet" things and I was like, "Did you misspell 'steal'? Because that seems like weird advice and also it's suspicious that an editor spelled something wrong. *Is this a test?*" and she was like, "No, 'stet' is the passive subjunctive, deriving from the active-voiced third-party subjunctive singular present, used to indicate that a marked change should be disregarded," and I was like, "No one knows your made-up language here, wizard," and she laughed but I was totally serious. So I looked it up and found out that basically if someone notes something on your page that's wrong you can just write "STET!" and it means "LET IT STAND." In my head it's always being shouted with authority by someone like Moses or Dumbledore, but in most situations in this book it just means "Yeah. I realize this part is fucked up. But it's fucked up *on purpose. Artistically.*" Usually it's a run-on sentence that would make an English teacher cut herself, or a word I made up just to see if I could get it in the dictionary on a bet, or a purposeful choice to use incorrect grammar because sometimes shit is funnier that way. "Stet" is my favorite verb, and it is the dryer setting I live my life in. Stet = Yes, it's fucked up *but I like it that way.*

Real-life examples of stet:

It's two o'clock in the late morning****** and I'm still in my pajamas and Victor keeps yelling at me about it, so I throw away all my pajamas and just start sleeping in comfortable dresses so I'll always be dressed appropriately.

Stet.

Binge-watching so much Netflix that it keeps asking me if I'm still alive with its judgy "ARE YOU *STILL* WATCHING?" message. *Stet.*

There are five foster baby rabbits in the guest room bathtub that Victor hasn't found yet. *STET LIKE THE WIND, MOTHERFUCKER.*

****** Victor just read this and left a note that says, "2 in the late morning isn't a thing. 2 in the afternoon is a thing." But two feels like late morning to me because I was up until dawn watching *The Great British Bake Off*. STET THAT SHIT, MOTHERFUCKER. (I think I just came up with the name of my next book.)

But sometimes you can't just stet shit away, because sometimes editing is more difficult than that, and that's why I collected a series of conversations I've had in the margins of my books with a variety of editors. Who are these editors? Sometimes they're professionals and sometimes they're my friends and sometimes they're family or my agent or actual *editor* editors, but one thing I suspect they have in common is that deep down they all hate me. Sure, they hug me and tell me they love me and give me hats made with the faces of roadkill animals, but I suspect if they do love me it's only because my constant mistakes ensure their job security and I make them feel better about themselves in comparison. My friend Karen refers to me as "Britney Spears in Mensa" in that I seem like a ditzy weirdo but most of the time I not only am in on the joke but am smart enough to recognize that I *am* the joke. And I am. But I suspect Karen reassesses when she looks through my rough drafts, because a box of owls understand semicolons better than I do and I refuse to learn enough about the Oxford comma to know which side of the battle I stand on. I can never remember if a period goes inside or outside of quote marks. I don't indent at the beginning of paragraphs. I intentionally misspell the word "goddamn" because it feels like if I don't spell it correctly then Jesus won't notice it. And I will *always* use two spaces after a period even though it's a clear sign that I'm over forty because that's how people who learned to type on weighty, horrible honest-to-Jesus typewriters were taught and if I stop it's like pissing on the grave of my seventh-grade typing teacher. And also, I don't want to stop.

Those aren't even the major things that got caught in editing though. These, however, are:

Editor: You wrote that Blackbeard kept severed heads in his closet but I can't confirm. Sources?

Me: It's a pretty well-known thing. From, like, books?

Editor: Can you give me a source?

Me: Okay, I just looked it up on the Internet and I can't find it either so *who is whitewashing Blackbeard's secret head collection?* Because someone is scrubbing the Internet. That's some patriarchal bullshit.

Editor: ?

Me: Wait. Hang on. Turns out it was *BLUEbeard* who kept all those decapitated heads in the closet. Not Blackbeard. But in my defense, they had the same last name so they're probably getting mistaken for each other all the time.

Editor: I don't think "Beard" was their last name.

Me: Well, agree to disagree.

Editor: You used the phrase "Charlie horse" but it should be "charley horse."

Me: But that's not how you spell "Charlie." Why is it spelled that way?

Editor: No one knows.

Me: THEN HOW DO YOU KNOW I'M WRONG? Someone spelled Charlie wrong in the 1800s and now I'm getting yelled at for it.

Editor: We can spell it wrong if you want.

Me: I just spilled all my tater tots on the floor. I can't make decisions right now. Go with your gut.

Editor: You're missing an antecedent.

Me: No, YOU'RE missing an antecedent.

Editor: What?

Me: Never mind. I've been drunking.

Editor: *drinking*

Me: Touché.

Me: Let's change "butt" to "buttonhole" here.

Editor: We can, but are you sure you want to do that?

Me: *Shit.* No, sorry. Autocorrect did that. I meant let's change "butt" to "*butthole.*" "Butthole" is funnier than "butt." Although "buttonhole" is sort of funny too. Should we say "buttonhole"?

Editor: I'll change it to "butthole."

Editor: You wrote, "You spend an hour talking about yourself and someone has to fake being fascinated by the minutia that is you." To be grammatically correct we should change "someone has to fake being fascinated by the minutia that is you" to "someone has to fake being fascinated by the minutiae that are you."

Me: *That can't possibly be right.*

Me: I need help with this sentence because I think it needs a semicolon but I don't know exactly how to place it.

Editor: You don't really need a semicolon in that sentence. I'll send a helpful link that shows you when and how semicolons work.

Me: Things I still don't understand; SEMICOLONS.

Editor: *Wow.*

Editor: When you run in a quote without setting it off with a comma, the pronouns and verbs agree with the overall sentence, so the "I" in the quote would be you, not Victor. This is technically a grammatically imperfect solution, but it avoids the issue of the reversed pronouns and seems to fit the flow of your writing.

Me: I'm so lost here. Honestly, you might as well be talking to my dog.

Editor: Alternatively, you can put the right pronouns in the quote in brackets: "[he'd] rather have [his] nuts cut off than have to listen to [me] talk about having three-ways with dead sheep."

Me: I'm embarrassed for both of us right now. I mean, more for me, obviously.

Editor: There's no hyphen in "monkey waiter."

Me: How do you know? They don't exist yet.

Editor: They have them in Japan.

Me: Clearly we need to hang out together more.

Editor: So was it THE Debra Messing that made the painting of the buttholes wearing Cosby sweaters?

Me: I don't know. The painting was signed by *A* Debra Messing, but I don't know if it was *THE* Debra Messing.

Editor: It might be safer legally to just drop this whole paragraph completely.

Me: Agreed. Also, some helpful advice: don't Google "Debra Messing's butthole." Now I have to figure out how to clear my Internet search history.

Editor: Noted.

Editor: You used the word "adverse" here but I think you mean "averse."

Me: I reject your authority.

Editor: So . . . do you want me to change it?

Me: Holy crap. I just looked it up and you're totally right. *Apparently I've been using the word "adverse" wrong for my whole life.* I thought I was adverse to change but turns out I'm *averse* to change because the first is a reaction and the second is a feeling? This would be easier to accept if I wasn't so adverse to change.

Editor: You're just doing it on purpose now, aren't you?

Me: Pretty much.

Me: I feel bad that there are so many errors that y'all keep finding. I feel like I'm wasting time leaving comments saying that you're right. From now on can I just leave a poop emoticon as shorthand for "Sorry I'm shitty at words"?

Editor: All drafts need corrections. This is very normal. Also, the poop image is an "emoji." An emoticon is a typographical display of facial representation using text only.

Me: Jesus, I can't even use poop correctly.

Editor: You switched from present tense to past tense here so we need to change so that the tenses match. I suggest you change "I was crazy" to "I am crazy."

Me: *Harsh.* And accurate.

Me: I know I spelled "weird" correctly here but it looks strange. All the other words with "ei" in them are pronounced like a hard A. "Vein." "Neigh." "Eight." So why isn't "weird" pronounced "wayrd"? Because the more I look at it the wronger it looks.

Editor: Now isn't a good time to point out that "wronger" isn't a real word, is it?

Me: If I got stabbed right now you'd find a way to fix this book without my help, right? Can we just pretend that happened and you can take over? Or do I need to be real stabbed?

Editor: It's gonna be okay.

Me: Did you just use the word "gonna"?

Editor: It hurt, but it seemed like you needed it.

Me: You're one of the good ones, you know.

Editor: There's no hyphen in the word "douchecanoe."

Me: Nope. You are wrong and I am willing to die on this hill. DON'T MAKE ME FLIP THIS TABLE.

Editor: Not sure how to edit this section. What is a chupacabra?

Me: Seriously? HOW DO YOU NOT KNOW WHAT A MEXICAN GOAT-SUCKING MONSTER IS? I guess now we're even.

Editor: You wrote "the possum clinging to my bush did furious acrobats" but I think you meant "acrobatics."

Me: Yeah. That sort of changes the story, doesn't it? The possum was NOT having sex with angry gymnasts in my bush. I'm pretty sure that's illegal in Texas. Thank you for saving me from myself.

Legal department editor: You can't legally say this book repels corpses.

Me: I can't legally trespass at unexpected funerals either but that doesn't mean it's not happening. Can we just add a note that says if someone finds a corpse stuck to this book they can mail the book, the corpse, and a legible receipt to me and I will happily refund their money?

Legal department editor: Probably not.

Audiobook editor: That's not how you pronounce [*INSERT SO MANY WORDS HERE*].

Me: That's because there are a lot of words that I've only read but never hear used. If I mess up pronunciation can we just add a note to the cover saying that's how they pronounce words in England? Say I'm using the queen's English. Or the king's? Whoever owns English now. Because it's not me. I can't even pronounce "hyperbolic" correctly. But everyone believes me when I say it's a British pronunciation 'cause those fuckers are fancy and it sounds like you're speaking American in cursive.

Audiobook editor: What about the people in England listening?

Me: I'm pretty sure they're used to us fucking up their words, so even if I mispronounce something they'll just be like, "Oh, that must be the *new* English. They just continue to destroy it a little more each decade. My God, this woman is progressive. I wonder how she says *lieutenant*." And the answer is that I don't because it's too confusing. The English fucked it up for me by adding sounds that aren't in the letters. It's like a practical joke they keep thinking we'll fall for.

Editor: We need to capitalize "Pegasus" throughout the book.

Me: They're awesome, but worthy of capitalization? You don't capitalize the word "unicorns" so why do we capitalize "Pegasus"?

Editor: There aren't Pegasuses. There's only one mythical creature whose formal name was "Pegasus." All the rest are just
winged horses.

Me: There's only one Pegasus? Like the Highlander? My whole
life feels like a lie.

In conclusion, editing is hell and will make you realize how incredibly stupid you are,******* but in the end it's for the best because
you learn new things and that's what books are for.

Even for the author.

Hell, especially for the author.

STET

*******I am currently editing this book and I was surprised at how often my editor had
written "PULL OUT QUOTE" in the margins, and I was like, "Oh my God, she hated
this. She's pulling out everything," but turns out that "pull out quote" is shorthand for
"This might be a good quote to pull out and promote when the book is marketed," and
this is *exactly* why I need an editor-to-author translator.

The First Satanic Ritual I Ever Saw

The thing I like the most about cooking is *absolutely nothing*. I mean, obviously some people must like it because cake keeps getting made, but cooking is a language I never learned, which is strange because both my parents cook, although in extraordinarily different ways.

My mother is an amazing cook and made do with whatever we had handy, which meant we ate a ton of fried deer nuggets. When we had money we'd have mashed potatoes and gravy, and when we didn't we'd shred stale white bread and pretend it was mashed potatoes. That sounds sort of pathetic but it was actually fucking delicious.

My father cooks as if each meal is an adventure, and in a way it is, because it's always sort of a surprise that we survive it. When I was eight he brought home an unexpected goat that he got in trade for taxidermy work or as a reward for saving someone from losing an arm from a snakebite. My mother refused to cook it because she wasn't going to stick a whole goat into her nice clean oven. My sister and I had noticed the goat in the bed of my father's truck and

named the goat Goaty Goaterson (we weren't very imaginative children) and had many short-lived dreams about what a great pet he'd
be until we realized that Goaty was dead and not just a very heavy
sleeper. My dad tried to convince us to tell our mom to cook the goat
but you don't eat things you've named, and eventually he sighed
and gave up. A few hours later he dug a large hole and buried Mr.
Goaterson in the backyard.

This seemed strange because my father is a realist, so I had
assumed he'd feed the goat carcass to whatever wild animals he'd
found and was currently nursing back to health. But it seemed as
if Mr. Goaterson must have made more of an impression, so I came
over to pat my father consolingly on the back and fashion a small
cross for the grave out of Popsicle sticks. My dad was already busy
gathering larger sticks himself, and I thought it was weird because he
never marked any of our pets' graves and I pointed out that he'd buried Monsieur Goaterson (we had more respect for the dead) almost
five feet away from our last dead pet (Squish the hamster) and then
my father explained that Goaty was *not* part of our pet cemetery
and that he was only burying the goat for the day, which is not how
burials work unless you're burying Jesus, but even he needed three
days and a tomb and frankly, *this goat was no Jesus*. Honestly, he was
barely even a goat by the time we met him, and I wondered if my
father had seen more in Goaty than we had or if he'd lost his mind
entirely. I didn't have a chance to ask because a half dozen of my
father's friends showed up and stood in a circle as they built a large
bonfire on top of the goat grave, and this was when I witnessed what
I assumed was my first satanic ritual.

I ran back inside to tell my mom that something terrible was happening and she explained that my dad had decided to make a "dirt
oven" and was roasting the goat in the ground. She also told me not

to eat Mr. McBastedInTheDirt, which was one of the most unnecessary pieces of advice she ever gave me.

I remember watching a lot of grown men stomping out the dry-grass fires that spread through our back lot and wondering if they knew that they were also stomping on all our dead hamsters and cats, who were now being lightly roasted as well. I don't think my father and his friends ate my other dead pets (mostly because they were probably fully mummified by then) but they were adventurous men with questionable decision-making skills, and if they did accidentally dig up a guinea pig with the goat I suspect they would have considered it jerky and at least tried it. There is a certain amount of nervy boldness that comes with eating something you disinterred from a pet cemetery, even if you did wrap it in tinfoil and allspice first.

This sort of thing was not really unusual at our house. My father loved to cook outside but having a barbecue was too pedestrian, so he'd often cook things—squirrels, deer, steak, more squirrels, unrecognizable parts of things—over a handmade fire. Often he'd rush excitedly inside the house with a large and dripping something on a fork, his hand under it as if to catch it if it suddenly came back to life, excitedly demanding, "TRY THIS," to my sister and me as we shook our heads vehemently and tried to hide in closets while my mother yelled, "HENRY, YOU ARE DRIPPING BLOOD ALL OVER THE CARPET." He'd look disappointedly at his boring family, who would never know the joy of outdoor cooking or the taste of groundhog and tetanus.

My sister and I never truly enjoyed the broiled chickens with full beer cans stuck up their internal cavities so that the beer would boil and steam into them through their buttholes, although it was interesting to watch the chickens seem to twerk awkwardly as they enjoyed the worst beer bong ever. Most children go through stages of refusing to eat lima beans or brussels sprouts, but we drew the line at eating anything we'd watched get a booze enema. My father would often claim that we didn't have enough imagination, but we were pretending that ripped-up bread was potatoes, so our imagination was already overtaxed. (Also, gravy on white bread is delicious. And possibly why we're all pre-diabetic.)

Our attitude was baffling to my father, who had been raised in the country with very old-world Czech parents who didn't believe in wasting anything. They made sausage at the kitchen table, grinding the meat and stuffing it into intestines that I would have thought looked like alarmingly giant condoms if I'd been old enough to know what condoms were. Instead I was just alarmed at the fact that we were still storing food in intestines when Tupperware existed. My grandmother said I was missing the point, because intestines are "crunchy and delicious," and I would have argued with her but 1) she was totally right, and 2) that same morning I'd watched her decapitate a chicken that unsettlingly ran out into traffic headless.******** The casual, easy way she ripped the head off was

---

******** Why did the chicken cross the road? Because your granny killed it too near the driveway and it didn't realize it wasn't really dead yet.

Side note on this footnote: Did you know that in the forties there was a chicken who lived perfectly normally for eighteen months without a head because the farmer axed off his noggin but missed his jugular and brain stem? They named him Miracle Mike and fed him milk with an eyedropper until he unexpectedly choked to death on his own snot, which is a pretty embarrassing way to die after being the kind of tough motherfucker who survives being decapitated by a man with an axe. I always wondered if the farmer didn't just try to kill it again because he thought it was immortal or because his kids named it after the "incident" and you can't eat things you name. Regardless, it seems the shared shame of the two would be uncomfortable since Mike was literally a walking reminder of that farmer's fucking up.

Footnote on the side note on this footnote: You know the joke "Why did the chicken cross the road? To get to the other side"? I didn't get that joke until last week. Like, I thought it was just one of those jokes like, "Why did the pig eat lunch? Because he was hungry," which Victor said isn't a joke, and I was like, "Yeah, I thought the point was that it's not funny." But then I saw a cartoon of the joke and the chicken was a ghost that had been hit

a product of life on a farm, but to me it was more of a reminder that maybe you shouldn't fuck with your badass grandma because you have no goddamn idea what she's actually capable of.

Happily, my father now has grandchildren who are far more adventurous than my sister and I ever were. They don't hesitate to try raw octopus or pig's feet or gizzards. They love the excitement that weeks spent with their grandparents bring. They've been warned not to drink the homemade moonshine and my mother keeps them away from anything too dangerous, but they appreciate the strange country life more than Lisa and I ever did (possibly *because* it is strange and unusual to them). They will hunt, cook, and take care of the animals that roam around the house that my sister and I grew up in, while she and I tell them to wash their hands after playing with the catfish and to close the door so the neighbor's wandering peacocks don't get in the house and shit everywhere while screaming like murder victims.

Last month I went back home for a week and my sister brought her kids down from California. We all stayed at my parents'. On the last day we went to a small piece of land my parents had bought recently when they sold the family farmland. It's just woods and cactus and it's made of Texas and sheep and deer. We settled on a hill that overlooks the land. My dad had set up a full Old West chuck wagon and a rock firepit, and we made a bonfire and the kids played in the dry creek bed and my sister and I agreed finally that perhaps my father was

---

by a car and he was like, "Worth it," and I was all, "OH MY GOD, THE OTHER SIDE = DEATH. THE CHICKEN IS SUICIDAL," and suddenly I understood the joke for the first time ever and now I'm wondering what other basic things I think I understand but really don't at all, and Victor says there are probably too many too count and I would argue with him but I'm still vulnerable from this chicken epiphany, and now I'm questioning everything, including how footnotes work.

onto something after all. That is, until we realized that there wasn't a toilet around for miles and there was too much cactus to squat without fear. But then my father proudly led us to an outhouse he and his grandson had put together using old barn wood. He pointed out the historical accuracy of the antique almanac nailed to the door to use as toilet paper and the sack of corncobs, and Lisa whispered, "What are the corncobs for?" and I was like, "Victorian tampons?" but turns out it's for wiping poop off your butt and that's why I'm never trying time travel. We decided that maybe we weren't quite as outdoorsy as we thought and figured we should just hold it, but then Lisa gave up because she hates urinary tract infections even more than peeing next to a box of questionable corncobs. My dad yelled, "DON'T FORGET TO USE THE SNAKE STICK," and then Lisa was like, "*I want to go home now.*" But my dad explained that you put a big stick into the poop hole and rattle it around first to make sure that there aren't snakes hiding inside, and Lisa and I immediately regretted not bringing adult diapers. After a few minutes of indecision she bravely used the snake stick but left the door open so that it wouldn't be dark, and when she hiked back down the hill to us she said, "I did not get bit by a snake, I no longer have to pee, and I watched a bunch of squirrels chasing each other through the cemetery." (There's a homemade cemetery. I forgot to mention that.) "That was"—she paused for the right words—"the prettiest pee I have ever had in my entire life." And so I went. And she was right. And my father was very proud.

Then I asked what would have happened if a snake *had* been in the hole, and my father just stared at me as we realized that basically we'd just have been riling up a poop-covered snake that had nowhere to go but up at the person shaking a stick at it, and I silently thanked God for plumbing.

I tried to make s'mores for the kids over the fire but managed to catch the marshmallows, the plastic bag, and the hem of my dress on fire before the rest of my family shooed me away and reminded me that cooking was not my strong suit. And they were right. In a way. But as the sun began to set I realized that all of this would make a wonderful family story we'd continue to tell each other. So perhaps I can't boil water without burning it, but I can cook up stories and memories and moments to be savored and devoured and experienced. They are equal parts delicious and strange and distasteful and unique. My concoctions are built from the traditions of my family and are crafted with love. They don't always work. Some are overdone and some are undercooked, but in the end they are mine. And they almost never give anyone botulism, so I think that counts as a win.

Damaged Good(s)

The year I started eighth grade there were three things you needed to be cool: add-a-beads, a leather notebook, and Swatch watches.

Technically you had to have at least three Swatch watches to be cool, and you had to wear them all on the same arm. I asked my mother for two Swatches for Christmas and she said I could have one if that was the one present I wanted. I explained that somehow just one was worse than none and she said that was great because I'd just saved her $35. If our generation had been smart we would have set them all to different time zones and explained that they were a symbol of global awareness, but according to my mother they were all set to the time we all lost our damned minds, because where the hell does a fourteen-year-old need to be that they even need a watch, much less three? She had a point, so instead I asked for—and was shocked to receive—the notebook and necklace for my Birthmas. (Birthmas is the tragic combined holiday that comes when you were born a few days after Christmas and everyone is too exhausted to care and everything you open during the holiday comes with a quick "That's for your birthday too" notation.) I wasn't complaining that year, though, because the leather notebook alone was about $75 and that was a fortune in our family.

I only recently realized that leather notebooks were not the harbinger of coolness in every American school when I was having a "remember when" conversation with my friend Laura and found out that she'd never heard of them, despite her being just as rurally Texan as me. Basically when you got into junior high you'd go to the local saddle store and they would make you a three-ring binder out of heavy saddle leather that you'd carry all through high school. Your name was hand-tooled onto the front of it like those belts everyone had in the eighties and it would be surrounded by saddle designs, and the whole thing zipped closed. It was pretty much unheard of to not have a leather notebook to carry through your high school career.

They smelled like cows and whatever cooking oil your mom had because you wanted it to look old and cool and oiling your notebook was a quick way to age it. My mom was furious when she saw that I'd scuffed the beautiful leather, but there was no way any of us would carry a pristine blond notebook around like some kind of weirdo. You were only cool if the Trapper Keeper made of a dead animal looked as if it had been handed down by dirty hippies, and the best way to give it that sheen of age was with what would have made it age naturally— the oils from handling it. Of course, hands aren't all that oily, so we all ingeniously worked with what we had, which meant smearing our oily, adolescent foreheads and noses onto our carcass-based notebooks *because that was the cool thing to do*.

I realize you're all shaking your heads at this ridiculousness but I suspect that's just because you didn't have a neighborhood saddle shop to make you school supplies. I bet, though, that you did tons of ridiculous stuff in the name of fitting in. Take, for instance, add-a-beads. In the eighties everyone in my school had an add-a-bead necklace, simple chains that you could add pea-sized gold beads to. They must have been expensive, because the richest girl in my grade only had seven beads. In order to prove that they weren't fakes you had to gently chew on the beads. They were made of such thin gold that they would dent easily, and so the permanent teeth marks would prove to everyone that they were real. It seems insane that the only way to make something special is to damage it forever, but we showed off those teeth marks as if they were diamonds. My mother was already pissed that I'd ruined my leather notebook by wiping my dirty face all over it, but when she saw that I'd intentionally chewed up the only real piece of jewelry I'd ever owned, she just stared at me and vowed to only buy already damaged goods for me from then on.

This is my sister's leather notebook because I am far too irresponsible to still have mine.

And I get it. It sounds ridiculous to covet damage, but honestly that had all started years ago in elementary school, when people were branded for fun. Again, I thought everyone did this, but apparently not all of you allowed the most popular girl in class to rub a pencil eraser across the back of your hand long enough that it ripped off several layers of skin and created a bloody mess that marked you as being cool enough to mutilate. It seems like there must have been a point to this, but I think the point was just "How dumb and/or bored are you?"

It was pretty idiotic to begin with, but then it turned into a thing where you would let your best friend brand you like some sort of fight club friendship bracelet. Eventually some kids got terrible infections and parents were pissed, and then the principal got involved and a rumor went around school that there would be an inspection and anyone with a brand would get licks (that's the word we used for spankings done with a paddle, and now I have even more questions as I'm writing this) and the person who branded you would also get licks. This was pretty terrifying because it got to the point where so many people had brands that not having one made it look like you were friendless, so in order to fit in you would intentionally give yourself leprosy-like lesions just to fit in. It sucks to be threatened with a beating for having a painful welt on your hand, but it's even worse to be threatened with a beating for disfiguring yourself because you're not popular enough for anyone else to mutilate you.

The principal did in fact bring us all in to chew us out and ended with "If everyone else jumped off a bridge, would you?" and that's a fair question, but he was asking young children who'd intentionally scarred themselves with brands like literal sheep out of peer pressure, so I think the answer was pretty obvious. Also, most of us had permanent scars from the playground slides that the community farmers made out of old sheet metal, so I'm not sure that he was really the best judge of what constituted safety.

I'd like to think that the reason we did such crazy things was to create our own unique spin on our lives . . . the handprint on the notebook that showed it was carried by us, the actual dental impressions we left in those previously immaculate golden beads, the early tattoos that showed our first childhood gang membership and terrible decision-making skills. But it's not really that.

If I look closer at these stories that make up my life, a strange theme emerges. It's the idea that something is only real if it's damaged.

I suppose it makes sense in a terrible sort of way. After all, we are changed by life . . . it puts its teeth in us, it leaves its handprints and marks and scars on us. And as much as we try to ignore those things, in the end they make us who we are. For good or for bad, we are changed and touched and broken and mended and scarred. And those marks (inside and out) tell a story. They tell *our* story.

Sometimes we hide them away, those injuries done by others (or, worse, by ourselves). We conceal them up our sleeves or jammed deep into pockets. We try to pretend that they never hurt at all. But it's a strange and meaningless action. Anyone who has lived would almost certainly understand and maybe even reveal their own hidden defects they've been hiding from the world as well. The world feels safer somehow if we share our pain. It becomes more manageable. And by sharing our pain, we inspire others to share theirs. We are so much less alone if we learn to wear our imperfections proudly, like tarnished jewelry that still shines just as brightly.

My House Is a Garbage Fire
Because I Clean It

Today our house tried to kill itself to escape me and I'm really trying not to take it personally.

Let me explain.

We have a central vacuum in our house. If you don't know what that is, then join the club, because it was new to me too. Apparently in the eighties, when our house was built, it was the thing to put pneumatic tubes in your walls to help you clean. Basically you just stick a vacuum hose into these holes in your walls and then your house becomes the vacuum. But did you know that you have to find the tank it dumps the dirt into and empty it? *Because I didn't know that.*

Related: my house was just on fire.

I mean, I guess I just assumed it emptied into some sort of sewer? Like a lint sewer? I don't really think about where the stuff I flush down the toilet pipes goes, so I assumed it was the same for the vacuum pipes, but apparently not, and that's why my whole house smells like four years of burnt cats right now and THIS IS EXACTLY WHY I DON'T CLEAN.

Victor and I had to open up the vacuum trash bucket thingy so that we could stop the fire, but the bucket hangs upside down from the garage ceiling and when we popped the latches that held it closed it exploded with smoldering garbage, which showered its fiery embers all over me, Victor, and the garage. Because OF COURSE IT DID. I don't know if you've ever had a trash-fire shower, but that's pretty much what this whole week has been like. Literally and figuratively. And it makes you rethink a lot of your choices . . . like my choice to ignore things I don't want to think about until they are literally on fire around me, which is probably the most American thing about me.

We couldn't vacuum up all the garbage in the garage because obviously the house vacuum was on strike, so Victor grabbed the Shop-Vac and I yelled, "OH, DON'T TOUCH THAT! IT'S FULL OF POOP," and Victor stared at me for a minute, and I was like, "It's not my poop," and then he sighed the sort of sigh that you do when your wife filled up your Shop-Vac with feces. Also, it might have been my poop.

Let me explain. Again.

Last week when Victor was out of town, Hunter S. Thomcat accidentally knocked an open bag of cat food into the sink and I used the Shop-Vac to suck up the food that was stuck down the drain and it worked really well, but did you know that sink pipes go to the sewer? And did you know that it's *really* easy to accidentally fill an entire Shop-Vac with stanky backwash raw sewage?

Because, again, *NO ONE TOLD ME.*

Honestly this whole week has been a lesson in sewers and vacuums and the repercussions of terrible decisions.

I'd considered leaving the now destroyed Shop-Vac out with the trash because I was never using it again, but I was afraid some well-meaning recycler would pick it up and carry home my big bag of shame sewage to his family, and I'm pretty sure that's how we all get cholera, so instead I left it in the garage until I could take it to the dump myself and then totally forgot it was there until the day I set fire to the house by vacuuming.

Victor was that level of mad where he was too angry (or impressed?) to speak, and he just glared at me as he slowly rolled the soiled Shop-Vac to the trash bin. Later I helpfully taped a note to the front of it that said, "HAS SHIT IN IT."

Then, while Victor went inside to probably file for divorce, I drove to the hardware store and bought a new Shop-Vac.

I used the vacuum to vacuum the vacuum, and I'm pretty sure that's how wormholes start, but something even worse than a wormhole happened. The Shop-Vac immediately clogged when I tried to suck eighteen pounds of old hair and burned garbage into it, and I had to call Victor to help, and he reversed the flow to clear the clog and it shot the garbage that had already been dumped on me on me again, *but this time with feeling*, and then I was like, "*Fuck this. I'm setting fire to the house. THE VACUUM HAD THE RIGHT IDEA.*"

Victor said I was overreacting but I'm pretty sure I'm not because in the last week I have ruined two vacuums, defiled a bathroom sink, and SET FIRE TO THE HOUSE BY DOING LIGHT HOUSEKEEPING.

On the other hand, I don't think I'm allowed to vacuum anymore, so I guess it all works out in the end. It still sucks though. Or blows. Maybe both.

And That's Why I Can Never Go Back
to the Post Office Again

"So I did what you told me to and returned that bag of stolen drugs and in exchange I got a big bag of dicks and that's why I can never go back to the post office again and all of this is your fault."

Victor glanced up from his computer and gave me that look you give someone who you suspect is trying to make up a reason to not go to the post office. I realized that maybe he needed proof so I explained, "And I would show you the penises but there was '*an incident*' and now they're all trapped in my car holes and I need you to help me dig them out so they don't melt in there or scar young children when I brake hard and dicks roll out at inopportune times."

Then Victor sighed and put his face in his hands and I was like, "I understand your frustration but maybe recognize that *I'm* the victim here and also this is all your fault because YOU'RE THE ONE WHO SAID I COULDN'T KEEP THE DRUGS IN THE FIRST PLACE."

And then I heard a strange man's voice say, ". . . So what happened to the penises?" and that's when I realized that Victor was on a conference call.

And I did feel bad, but 1) DOOR LOCKS AND MUTE BUTTONS EXIST, VICTOR, and 2) if I were him I would have immediately said, "I'm not sure who said that but that sounds like a very serious concern that we should table for offline discussion," and gone on with the call, but he totally didn't.

I felt a little bad, but I was pretty sure the people on the call were invested at that point, so I continued. Because I'm a people-pleaser.

(Several people reading this have asked me what "car holes" are, and duh . . . they're holes in your car. Like that black hole between your seat and the gearshift that all your French fries and dropped phones fall into. And where most of my penises currently were.)

"So remember yesterday when I picked up all my packages at the post office and one of them had a bunch of pills in it and you were like, 'You get the weirdest fan mail. Don't take pills from strangers, blah blah blah,' but then I realized that the post office had put the wrong label on the package and it was for the lady in the next PO box and you said I had to go back and return the mail even though I hate to talk to people because 'someone could die without their medicine.' So I did but on the way there the post office called me and said that the lady with the pills accidentally got one of my packages and she'd brought it back."

"Because she's a good person and that's what normal people do," Victor interrupted interruptingly. (Spellcheck is saying "interruptingly" isn't a word because I guess it's never spent time with Victor before. Also, it stopped me in the middle of writing this in a totally interruptingly way. *Way to disprove your point, spellcheck.*)

I explained that I suspected she'd returned my package less

because she was a better person than me and more because she probably opened the box of dead prairie dog that I'd been waiting for *forever* and mistakenly thought it was a threat instead of a gift.

Then Victor said, "I don't even know which question to ask first," and I was like, "Is it '*Who on earth would think a dead prairie dog is a threat?* ' Because that is a pretty good question honestly, but it's *not* just an anonymous box of dead rodent. It's a prairie dog dressed like Daenerys Targaryen, so it's pretty obvious that a lot of love went into it."

Then I realized that Victor's coworkers were very quiet and might not understand the reference, so I loudly explained at the phone, "Daenerys Targaryen is the Mother of Dragons and the true heir to the throne," and then Victor said that was literally the last thing that needed clarification regarding this whole conversation, because I guess everyone has HBO now.

But he was probably right, so I further clarified that the prairie dog was taxidermied, not just like a fresh corpse dressed up in tiny people clothes. That would be weird, and I agreed that people would be confused.

(Victor later said that was *not* why anyone was confused and only made things more baffling for everyone, but I don't know anyone who wants a limp prairie dog corpse in a fancy dress and tiny wig unless they're into some really kinky shit that I don't want to know about, but I'm not judging too much because, hello, *I have dicks stuck in my car holes*.)

"So *anyway*, I had to take the pills back because if I didn't then technically I think that counts as stealing drugs, and since it happened at a post office it'd probably be a federal offense, and then I'd end up in jail for life just because I didn't want to make small talk with the mail clerks. Are you still with me?"

Victor: "I mean . . . *in theory.*"

"So I went in and gave the clerk the package and I apologized for opening it, and he said that the other lady did the same thing and he handed me this sack, and I was like, *Who ships a prairie dog in a sack?* and I thought maybe I'd said it out loud because he looked at me really weird but then I realized he was probably really looking at me *because he'd just handed me a big bag of dicks.*"

Then Victor stared at me and I realized that I shouldn't say "dicks" on a business call, so I said, "Penises, I mean. A big ol' sack filled with a dozen small squishy penises. And they have smiley faces painted on them and their balls are their feet, I think? They're like those squishy stress toys that kids love, except these are penises and they're the size of a big toe. Also, they're very well made because they don't stink like most of them do. The squishy toys, I mean. Not penises. Yours smells fine." And then I whispered, "Shit, I just told everyone on the phone that your penis smells fine," and I felt like I should apologize, but also it's sort of a compliment? But then Victor was like, "Yeah, I disconnected that call right after 'dicks in your car holes,'" and at first I felt insulted but then I was like, "Good call," and moved to high-five him but he totally didn't high-five me back.

"*Aaanyway*," I continued, "they'd been waiting all day to give me this open bag of penises, so all the people working there were like, 'THAT'S THE PENIS LADY,' and the bag didn't have a note or a return address so I basically got an anonymous bag of genitals and I don't even know if it's supposed to be an insult. Because usually if someone says, 'HAVE A BAG OF DICKS,' that'd be rude, but these are kind of adorable so it's hard to say and I would show you them except that I had an accident."

Victor picked his head up off the desk. "Wait—did you wreck the car? Is this just your way of distracting me from wrecking the car?"

This was an extremely rude and also very valid question, because that totally sounds like something I'd do, but I explained that I had to slam on my brakes because there was a mattress on the highway and the bag hit the dashboard and dicks exploded everywhere and a bunch rolled under the seats. The penises were the only casualties, and I thought about pulling them out before they rolled further under the seats, but you always hear about people having wrecks because they're looking for a CD on the floorboard and I can't even imagine having to explain to the insurance adjuster that I'd run into a ditch because I was distracted by pulling penises out of my car holes. Victor agreed that that would be awful. Maybe not for the same reason.

"Thanks for asking if I'm okay, by the way," I added.

He took a deep breath. "Sorry. Are you okay?"

"NO I'M NOT, BECAUSE THERE ARE DICKS STUCK IN MY CAR HOLES AND EVERYONE AT THE POST OFFICE THINKS I BUY TINY DILDOS IN BULK."

"Right," Victor said. "Because *that's* the real issue here."

"And now the people at the post office probably think that I have a tiny vagina, and now every time I see them I'm going to want to defend my vagina and be like, 'I know you didn't ask out loud but I can assure you that my vagina is much roomier than you think.'"

Victor rubbed his temples. "I'm not sure that's something to brag about."

"And then when I was in the parking lot I did an Instagram video explaining the whole dick debacle but while I was pulling out my penises and putting them on the dashboard a guy walked by and just stared at me while I was shooting a video of me playing with my penis in the car and that's why I can never go back to the post office again."

Victor suspected this was all just a ploy so I'd never have to go to the post office, but he still helped me dig the penises out of the car, because apparently they're very melty in a hot car, like lipsticks or crayons or dogs. (Not that dogs are melty. They just shouldn't be left in hot cars.)

Later a woman saw my Instagram video and commented, "Oh, I sent you those as a gift! Aren't they awesome?" and yes, they actually are.

In fact, I enjoyed them so much that I put a handful in my purse to give to my friend Maile the next time I saw her. But then I saw a snake in my garage slithering toward my open door (not a euphemism) and I wanted to scare it away but not hurt it, so I started whacking its path with my purse to make it turn around, but my purse was still open so I was leaving a trail of purse debris behind me like Hansel and Gretel if Hansel had used tiny penises instead of bread crumbs. And the snake grudgingly went outside. I tried to get a video of it for Instagram but it was hard not getting any dicks in the frame. Then I tiptoed back into the house because it was dark and I was afraid the snake would dart under my feet and I would step on it.

Then Hailey opened the garage door because she'd heard all of the commotion and was like, "Why are you tiptoeing away from a snake and why are there so many penises on the floor?" and that was a good question, but technically it might have helped scare the snake away because maybe it looked like I was carrying around a bunch of snake heads like some kind of crazy snake cutter-upper.

Later Instagram informed me that the snake was not venomous

and was incapable of murder.******** Most readers were mainly concerned about the wording of my caption, which read:

"I just used my purse to chase this snake out of the house but I didn't kill it and I need you to tell me it's not poisonous so I don't regret not using the shovel. Thanks. Also, a penis fell out of my purse when I was lightly whacking it and now my child has questions. JOIN THE CLUB, KID. PS: It was very small and nonaggressive. The snake, I mean."

And that's why I can't go to the post office again.

PS: Remember when we were at the chapter about the cock-chafer on the sidewalk? And now there are penises outside my garage. This is a weird theme for a book, y'all, but it's an accidental one because I didn't choose for any of this to happen to me. I'm pretty sure it's a message from God telling me I need to leave the house more. Or less. But either way, the post office is out.

PPS: Hisstopher Columbus (so named because he was trying to discover my house even though I already lived there) is fine and I saw him this morning in the yard, but he was next to the tree that always has that owl in it and now I'm afraid for him, but I didn't want to pick him up so I just stood outside stomping my feet to scare him to a safer part of the yard. My neighbor drove by and it totally looked like I thought I was Godzilla. I wanted to explain that I was trying to save Hisstopher Columbus from owls, but I figured that would just make it worse.

******** A more accurate breakdown: 75 percent of Instagram said it was a helpful snake that should be cherished, and 25 percent screamed, "DANGER NOODLE. BURN THE HOUSE TO THE FOUNDATION AND SALT THE EARTH." Almost 100 percent thought I'd buried the lede and wanted to know more about the penises, and that's why this chapter exists.
You're welcome.

I Am a Magpie

I collect things. Like magpies and ravens, I pick up shiny, strange things and surround myself with them. Marbles. Glass animals. *Scrabble* tiles. Buttons.

Buttons are my favorite.

Which is strange because I don't sew. I grew up in a house with a mother who sewed though, so maybe that's where it comes from. Once, years ago, I saw a photo of a jar of shiny mother-of-pearl buttons and I could almost hear the noise it would make if I could run my hands through them. The same noise I heard as a child as my mother ran her fingers through buttons looking for just the right one to make my dresses. From the moment I saw that image I was a button collector.

At first I only collected white buttons. Then I got a jar for pearl buttons. Then one for black buttons. I graduated from jars to fishbowls as my collections accumulated. I'd run my hands through the cold buttons and listen to the soft clink and be transported to another time. I'm like Scrooge McDuck when he dives into his gold coins, except that my collection is fairly worthless. There are no special, rare buttons to sell, but they're special to me.

I mainly pick them up in thrift stores or antique stores or on eBay. New buttons are expensive and come stapled to a card. Old buttons are in crumbling boxes or mason jars, forgotten. The collecting of buttons is a bit of a lost art. They were once utilitarian but still ornamental. When my grandmother was young every woman she knew sewed her own clothes. They had fabric and pinking shears (the kind you'd later steal to give yourself terrible bangs when you were seven years old) and thimbles and needle threaders and brown tissue patterns and bric-a-brac. And buttons. Some new—bought and still on the cards—and some snipped off old clothes to use again. Buttons last longer than clothes. Longer than people.

Lately I've found my favorite buttons at estate sales, in those old houses whose owners have fled (either voluntarily or not) and that are filled with strange things the owners' family (if they have any) doesn't want. There are always sewing boxes. Sometimes the woman was a quilter. Sometimes an embroiderer. Sometimes a seamstress. But always there are buttons. The boxes of sewing materials and buttons are left abandoned on a side table. People don't sew like they used to. They throw away the extra buttons that come tagged with new shirts, knowing that either they or the shirt will likely wear out before the buttons.

I buy the sewing boxes and take them home to dig through them like they're treasure boxes. I separate the buttons by color. I snip away the thread that still clings to them. I will find long dark hairs in the older compartments. I will find gray ones on the top. And in that way I can chart the life of a woman growing older over her sewing box. I see the smaller needles and rusted thimbles and older buttons (some cracked and worn) on the bottom, and newer things like magnifying glasses and larger scissors on the top. I see the progression of time from the dusty pastel Easter colors of children's clothes, to the large seventies mustard and avocado buttons, to the neon plasticky buttons of the eighties.

I have often found tiny surprises hidden in those sewing boxes. A black carved horse the size of my fingernail. A coin from another country the owner may have visited. An inch-tall white porcelain baby. A black and white photo of a couple in front of a honeysuckle-covered house. Were they tucked in by children who wanted her to find them later as a surprise? Mementos? Things she tossed inside to keep away from the cat? I don't know, but I ask myself as I hold them and imagine her life. At a certain point it stops. The collecting of buttons and bric-a-brac. Perhaps she stopped sewing. Gave up. Died. But the buttons remain. They tell a story she didn't even know she was writing.

I take the parts I don't use (the needles and thread and thimbles) and put them away to resell one day to someone who collects such things. The buttons I sort out and clean and admire and then drop into my giant fishbowls.

I run my hands through them and see some of my favorites turn up. A gold button from a military uniform. A red button from the sixties shaped like a lamb. A white button made from a seashell. I remember where I got many of them. I remember who I was with and how they helped me pore over the tins of buttons at antique stores looking for the best and strangest ones. Suddenly seeing the beauty in them. Seeing the history. Wondering who hung on to them. Who wore them. Who kept them for projects that never came. Our fingers run through the buttons and we remember the women we never knew.

One day I will be gone and I can't imagine that anyone in my family (who are all magpies themselves with their own too-large collections of strange ephemera) will want my buttons. In my mind's eye I can see them for sale after I'm gone. Giant bowls of buttons on a card table. Most people won't even see them and will look past them . . . but some will stare at them and wonder what type of person would collect fishbowls of buttons sorted in such strange ways. Some will wonder what the story was, and some will make up their own. But I believe that one person will pause, and look, and then shove their hands deep into the cool, candy-colored buttons, and the soft, tinkling tintinnabulation will bring them back to a memory they'd almost forgotten and they will take home a fishbowl of memories and wonder why they ever bought it and how they lived without it. And I will be part of that story. Others came before me. Others will come after. The buttons will outlive us all.

I am a magpie.

But I am not alone.

Up Divorce Creek Without a Paddle (Because the Guide Didn't Trust Me Not to Push Victor Overboard with It)

Ten years ago Victor and Hailey and I took a group kayak tour. Hailey sat in between us as we paddled out under the stars through a cypress-tree-lined bayou in Puerto Rico that led to a bioluminescent lake, which literally glowed when our paddles glided through the water. It sounds like a magical fairy tale but only because the fantasy of the tour didn't take into account that Victor couldn't steer because his arm was in a cast, that Hailey was terrified of the dark, and that I am completely night-blind and was not able to see even a foot in front of me. I made up for the fact that I couldn't see with sheer determination and rammed us over and over into the walls of the bayou, where tree spiders would be knocked free and would shower down into our clothes.

Other couples might have used this as a team-building experience or laughed it off, but Victor continually screamed, "PADDLE LEFT," while I screamed back, "THAT IS LITERALLY ALL I

AM DOING," and Hailey would throw up on her lap from motion sickness and the guide would sigh and paddle back to dislodge us from the trees and then we'd immediately do it again. Eventually the guide just took our paddles away from us, hooked our kayak to his, and dragged our angry American asses into the open water. Later I discovered that when Victor said to paddle left, he meant I should paddle on the right so that we could go left, and that is the dumbest fucking thing I've ever heard and it made me really glad that he wasn't with Sandra Bullock during her *Bird Box* years because she'd probably be dead now.

Honestly I'm surprised we survived what we now lovingly refer to as "Divorce Creek," but this was just one of so many times when I was assured something would be amazing but it turned out to be something else altogether.

Take prom, for example. Everyone tells you that you *have* to go because otherwise you'll regret it and that "prom is what memories are made of!" But what no one tells you is that not all memories are good ones. The strongest memory I have about my prom experience is all the blood. This is not a *Carrie* reference. From what I've seen on TV, most high schools raise money for prom by selling tickets, but at our rural Texas high school you were not allowed to go to your prom unless you worked Dance Chicken, the annual fundraising event that involved gutting, roasting, and selling hundreds of whole chickens. Basically in order to attend your first formal dance designed to make you feel like a princess, you had to first spend a day in the backyard of the local church preparing buckets of freshly slaughtered birds.

My mom was the cafeteria lady at my school, so she volunteered to help. She tried to teach all of us how to remove the neck and the stuff inside the body, and I was like, "First off, *what?* Secondly, *no.*" She explained that the stuff inside the chicken's butthole was called "the innards" but I'm pretty sure she was just guessing, because "innards" is technically the name for anything inside something else and she probably just called them that because she didn't know what in the hell they were either. Then we had to pop out the kidneys and pull off the neck bones and I lasted about five minutes before I threw up my own innards and was relegated to stirring cauldrons of boiling barbecue sauce for the rest of the day.

We made over eight hundred chickens that day but there wasn't enough room to store them all in the warming area of the church kitchen, so we split them at the breast to lay them flat and then stacked them in towering chicken piles, like Jenga but with carcasses. The last people to pick up their food were given chickens squished so flat we could have fit them in pizza boxes.

There is a picture in my yearbook of my mother ripping things out of chicken buttholes with the two most popular girls in my class, and I think that's the best representation of my whole high school career.

My actual prom night consisted of me in a blood-colored dress made by my aunt Wanda. I lasted almost fifteen minutes in the dance hall before I realized that almost every song was a two-step and I'd never learned how to dance. Then I locked my keys in my car, which was the highlight of the whole damn night.

Life is full of these moments that are supposed to be amazing but end up being questionable at best. I often wonder if it's because we build them up as being so important and so they can never measure up. I think that's part of it, but honestly I suspect that the people who made up all the milestones that are supposed to be important are psychopaths. Or maybe they just think that since they had to live through them everyone else should too. Or maybe people really do believe that your wedding day is the best day of your life or that childbirth is only worthwhile if you are entirely sober and in a pond filled with swans. These, I feel sure, are the same people who love weeklong class reunions and baptisms and skydiving and extra-long wedding speeches and accidentally harvesting tree spiders as your husband screams at you and your shoes fill up with vomit.

My point is, don't let other people set your expectations for what is or isn't important in life, because so often the best moments are the ridiculous laughter at funerals or the mundane but lovely conversations with family or the unexpected friends you make in prison.

When I was writing this, Victor told me that I'd forgotten to mention the best part of Divorce Creek. I had no idea what he was talking about. He reminded me that when we got into the open water our guide explained that the glowing water was caused by bioluminescent plankton called "dinoflagellates," but he pronounced it "dino flatulence," and after the third time I couldn't stop laughing. Then Hailey started laughing. And then Victor. And then everything was okay.

On the way back through the bayou we saw other couples on their way to the open water who were paddling in circles and stuck in the trees and screaming at each other, and we chuckled knowingly at the ridiculously young and unsophisticated us of thirty-two minutes ago and we felt very proud and wise for surviving it all and coming out stronger on the other side.

Maybe you have to go through Divorce Creek to get to the good part. Maybe the good part is just knowing that you made it through. Maybe the reason my memory of pulling necks off of chickens is stronger than the memory of actually attending prom is that it was a good moment to be cherished.

Actually, *fuck that*. It was awful and prom was boring as shit, and to this day I can't touch a raw chicken without dry-heaving. But I am still glad I went because otherwise there would always be a question in my head that maybe I'd missed something important and life changing. And in a way, I got something better than the magic prom moment you see in movies. I got the realization that what works for me may not work for you and vice versa. I got the knowledge that I get to decide what is an important milestone or memory and what is not. And I got a built-in excuse to never cook chicken for the rest of my lifetime. And *that* has made all the difference.

Eclipse (Not the *Twilight* Book.
The Other Kind.)

Do you want to hear a story about how I almost went blind because of diarrhea rats? Of course you do.

Here it is.

This year everyone was talking about the fact that there was a solar eclipse coming. Where we are in Texas, only about 70 percent of the sun would be eclipsed by the moon, but I was still very excited about it. Sadly, all of the special glasses designed to let you look at the sun were sold out in my city because I'm a procrastinator, and also Texas is so boring that staring at the sun for two hours was apparently a much bigger draw than anyone had expected. I went to the Internet to see what was the safest thing that was still available to stare at the sun behind, and the suggestions were the safety glasses that they were sold out of and a set of floor-to-ceiling blackout curtains (which I thought was overkill but I appreciated the caution). Victor later pointed out that the curtains probably showed up because their brand name was "Eclipse," but I prefer to think that Google is becoming sentient and learning sarcasm from me.

Helpful people on Twitter suggested that I go to a hardware supply store and buy a welder's mask to watch the eclipse through, but Victor refused to buy me one because he said it was dumb and a waste of money. I assured him that it would be fine, and that's when he told me that not only should I *not* stare into the sun (STOP TELLING ME WHAT TO DO, VICTOR) but I also had to keep Dorothy Barker inside during the hours of the eclipse because he'd heard that animals will stare at the eclipse and go blind. That doesn't really make sense, because no one has ever told dogs not to look at the sun and you don't see them just staring at it every time they go outside, plus there have been solar eclipses since the sun was invented and we didn't end up with a bunch of blind neighborhood squirrels falling out of trees. I told Victor that if he really wanted Dottie to be safe we should get her a tiny dog-sized welding mask, but he just rolled his eyes. Probably he was right to be doubtful, because Dottie had refused to wear the tiny Uncle Sam beard and hat I bought for her for the Fourth of July and that shit was *adorable*, so having her gratefully wear a tiny welder's mask around the neighborhood was maybe expecting too much from her.

Now, you might point out that I could have gone and bought a welder's mask myself, but no, I couldn't, because 1) I didn't want to because I'm lazy, and 2) I'd had an altercation with the people at our hardware store and now I can never go back there. This is that story:

Last week I was in my backyard when I was attacked by three small bears.

I'm going to pause here because when I wrote this sentence spell-check underlined "I was attacked by three small bears" like it didn't even believe me and I was like, *YOU DON'T KNOW MY LIFE,*

SPELLCHECK, but turns out it was just questioning my grammar rather than being concerned for my well-being:

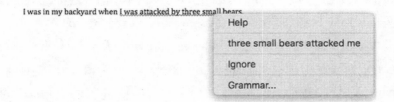

I realize I was being defensive but it's hard to be objective because I'm still emotionally distraught from being assaulted by eight wolverines. And I realize that I just changed my story, and that's because it was dark and I was scared and I couldn't tell what they were because they were so fast. Also, they were really just small rodents, but if I'd started the story with that sentence you'd have dismissed my fear level, and trust me when I say that *they scared the shit out of me*. I'm still not sure what they were but there were several of them and they ran from one bush to another near my feet and Dorothy Barker's eyes were enormous and she was like, "WHAT THE SHIT IS THAT? PICK ME UP, LADY," and I get it because I totally wanted someone to pick me up too, but also I was thinking, "Aren't tiny dogs like you *bred* to kill rats?" and she looked back at me like, "You're thinking of rat terriers. I'm a papillon. *I'm fucking French, bitch. WE DON'T EAT RATS.*" And she had a point but stop being so goddamn uppity, dog. Just this morning you shit in the yard and stole a sandwich out of the trash, so maybe we can drop the pretentiousness.

We hurried back inside, and from the kitchen window I could see one still scurrying around, and it looked smaller than a rat but larger than a mouse. Like a giant hamster if a hamster had a rat tail. (A literal one, I mean. Not the unfortunate haircut your weird cousin had in the eighties.) And a small part of me wanted to lure them inside and train them and dress them up in little costumes, but that urge was slightly smaller than my urge to involuntarily scream and run quickly away from them before they touched me (which, incidentally, is almost exactly how I feel about human babies—other than my own).

Victor was out of town on business (*because of course he is when a plague of rats strikes*) so I called the exterminator and said, "I think I have . . . lawn gerbils? Is that a thing?" Turns out that is not a thing according to Denise, the woman who sends the exterminators out on calls. I described the creatures and Denise was like, "Oh, guuurl, you got rats," and I protested but she was not having any of what she seemed to assume was my I'm-too-good-for-rats attitude.

"But they're smaller than rats," I offered weakly, and she very plainly said, "Well, then you've got teenage rats. You know they aren't born full-sized, right?" And then I might have screamed, "THIS STUFF NEVER HAPPENED WHEN OBAMA WAS PRESIDENT," and she was all, "Um . . . ma'am?" and I took a deep breath and apologized and explained that I had a lot of stuff going on right now and she was like, "Okay. *Whatever, crazy,*" but in a very nice way that made me think she probably missed Obama too, but not so much that she thought he'd made rats extinct while he was president.

Denise explained that she could send someone to help but that it would be expensive and that it's hard for them to catch rats outside, and helpfully suggested that I might want to try getting some rattraps and taking care of the problem myself. And I was grateful for the advice; however, I explained, "But I don't want to kill them. Can't you just live-trap them and take them far away? Like witness protection?"

"Witness protection for *rats*? *No.*" She sighed with a combination of exasperation and pity that made me think she'd probably never seen *The Secret of NIMH.* "We do that for possums or raccoons and such, but we're not going to trap and relocate *rats*. That would just cause problems for someone else. *Nobody wants rats.*" And that's probably true but technically it would create more business for them if they just relocated unwanted rats all the time, although it would be a very shitty and unethical business model and I mentally applauded them for not taking that route.

Denise told me that there were several different methods, including a poison that dehydrates the rats and makes them leave your house to look for creeks and rivers, but that we'd need to make sure that we closed all of our toilets because "sometimes they'll try to climb in there to drink," and I was like, "SO THEN YOU HAVE *TOILET RATS*? WHAT THE FUCK, DENISE? YOU JUST DESCRIBED A PHOBIA I DIDN'T EVEN HAVE UNTIL NOW." Also, I can only assume the poison makes the rats dehydrated by giving them diarrhea and was invented by the people who answered the age-old question of: "How can we make rats *more* unsanitary?" It also might explain why the rats want to get to the toilet so desperately. But Denise calmly explained that that method was really more for rats that were already in your house and that maybe since they were outside they'd go further away, but the bush they'd run into was right next to our pool so basically I'd have a lot of plague rats with the scoots floating around in my pool, and frankly that seemed worse for everyone involved.

Denise asked if I had any food or birdseed outside that was attracting them, and that felt a bit like victim-blaming, but I explained that I certainly didn't have anything outside they'd want to eat, and that's when she calmly mentioned that *RATS EAT DOG POOP*. WTF. At this point I considered that Denise was just fucking with me but she seemed to know her stuff, and this dog-poop revelation super grossed me out, because *ew*, but also it gave me pause, because that seems sort of beneficial? Like when you find a snake in your yard and you don't kill it because it eats worse snakes? So I asked the lady if I could just make the rats into outside pets who eat all the dog poop and she was like, "NO. THEY WILL GET IN YOUR HOUSE AND CHEW UP YOUR WIRES," but probably not if I made them a dollhouse out of peanut butter crackers on the back porch, and I could hear the lady shaking her head and she was like, "Just get some rattraps and see if you can catch them yourself. It's not hard. Bait them with cherry Starbursts because for some reason they really like cherry Starbursts," and I was all, "*I* REALLY LIKE CHERRY STARBURSTS," and then suddenly the rats got human to me. But then I remembered that I actually like *strawberry* Starbursts and that the cherry ones taste like poison, so I related to them less, but then I thought that if I *did* make friends with the rats they could eat all my leftover cherry Starbursts and poop. (Not my poop. The dog's poop. Not sure if that clarification is necessary.) You can see my predicament.

The pest control lady could *not* see my predicament. I assume because she didn't have my imagination or my access to tiny rat-sized clothing.

I went to the hardware store and realized that the only thing more embarrassing than buying tampons is buying rattraps. Probably the only thing worse than that would be buying rat tampons. Meaning tampons for rats, obviously. Not tampons made out of rats. That would be insane and probably something that one of those wilderness-survival-show guys would come up with. "Bleeding out your vagina? No problem! Stick an absorbent rat up there!" You're definitely getting toxic shock from that.

The guy in the pest control section saw me pulling out a large live trap ("Fits raccoons to rats!") and he was like, "You got a marmot?" But he said it really casually, as if he'd said, "You got a light?" and it was disconcerting because I don't know, *DO I HAVE A MARMOT?* And I explained that I wasn't sure but I thought maybe it was lawn gerbils, and he explained those weren't a thing, and we quickly came to an impasse.

When I got home I prepped the trap and I'd forgotten the Starbursts, so instead I baited it with peanut butter, and it worked too well, because I turned my back for a second and Hunter S. Thomcat was stuck inside and looking ashamed (but not too ashamed to stop eating the peanut butter) and I was like, "*You literally saw me set up this trap, you dummy,*" but technically cats can't stay out of boxes and this was a box with food in it, so I suppose I might be the stupid one, but at least I knew that it worked and also that if you give Hunter peanut butter he looks like he's talking and you can send a video to your husband of his seeming to say, "HELP ME, DADDY. I'M TOO PRETTY FOR PRISON."

Then Victor texted me and was all concerned because I guess it makes him cranky when I'm incredibly responsible and then he was like, "I'm not sure what's 'responsible' about sending me videos of the cat in a rattrap," but that was just for a second and it was FOR YOUR BENEFIT, VICTOR. Plus, I pointed out that Hunter might have learned something from his time in prison because maybe he was scared straight (disclaimer: he learned nothing and immediately tried to push his way back in when I baited the trap again), but Victor said that he was more concerned about the fact that I'd just left a large live trap in the backyard and texted:

"Did you forget that we have a skunk that hangs out in the backyard occasionally?"

And I was like, "*Of course I didn't forget that.* Stop insulting me. I've got it covered." But internally I was like, *GODDAMN IT, I DID FORGET THAT*, and suddenly I regretted living in Texas.

I called animal control and asked if they could come pick up a trapped skunk and they were all, "I mean, maybe? Where are you?" and I explained that it was a hypothetical skunk and that I wasn't even trying to catch it but I was looking for lawn gerbils and I needed a backup plan if the skunk tried to cockblock me, and the technician was like, "Wait. Start over. Are you high right now?" and I wasn't and was a little insulted but I explained it again more slowly and he was like, "First of all, your lawn gerbils sound a lot like rats. People don't 'live-trap' rats. *Because they're rats.* Second, if you accidentally catch a skunk, just get a big tarp and hold it up in front of you and then drop it over the trap," and I said, "Like when you're in the splash zone at a Gallagher show?" and he was like, "You've lost me again," and I offered, "You know, with the watermelons and the sledgehammer?" but there was just silence and I was like, "THE SUSPENDERS GUY?" and he just said, "Why don't you just call us if you catch something?" and then I remembered that not everyone is as old as I am and I hung up.

Turns out, though, that it didn't matter, because the trap kept getting sprung but was always empty of gerbils and peanut butter in the morning, so I was like, *My lawn gerbils are also ghosts, obviously.* Then I was told that the trap was too big "because rats can squeeze through crazy tiny holes and under doors and here's your new phobia," so I went online to order *another* trap but I reset the old one just in case and an hour later it was still open and unsprung BUT THERE WAS SOMETHING IN IT. Not an alive something.

A small, shiny star. Inside the trap.

And I wanted to get it out because *why was it even there and how did someone put it there without setting off the trap*, but also I didn't want to touch it because what if the rats left it and wiped hantavirus all over it to pay me back for trying to evict them? I looked for garden

I realize this is an awful photo but in my defense, it's hard to take a good picture when you're wearing slippery opera gloves and holding the bait that fairies might be using to curse you.

gloves but all I could find was satin opera gloves from an old Halloween costume, so I was basically dressed up super fancy to put my hand in a rattrap that had possibly been hacked to catch *me*.

It was a plastic, shiny star smaller than a penny, and I managed to get one unfocused photo of it before it slipped out of my gloved fingers and dropped into the succulent bushes that the rats were hiding in. I used a stick to try to move the plants so I could find the star but the whole time I was thinking, *What if this was their plan all along? What if they drag me down to their lair and this is where all the missing people and socks go?* But in the end I couldn't find the star or the ghost rats and it was really hot, so I gave up.

Hailey thought it was fairies or that the rats were leaving a present to repay me for all the free peanut butter, like tiny Boo Radleys with limited means. (Boo RATleys. Fuck. Now I want a rat named Boo Ratley.) Victor suggested it was a tiny throwing star left as a threat because I didn't use Starbursts. In the end it didn't really matter what I used, because I found out that our backyard squirrel (Squirrelly Temple) had learned how to dismantle the traps and would scoop out the peanut butter like a tiny bandito.

I spent yesterday literally building a better rattrap, only to watch this fucker pull the trap five feet into the bushes, jump on it, pry the back off, and pull out the peanut butter, and now SHE'S FUCKING PICKING HER TEETH WITH THE HANDLE SHE BROKE OFF.

The last time, Squirrelly Temple ripped off the back of the trap AND CARRIED IT AWAY WITH HER SO I COULDN'T SEAL IT BACK UP. So basically she converted the trap into a squirrel feeding system and now she keeps glaring at me like, "Why haven't you refilled this shit? IT IS *EXHAUSTING* STEALING FROM YOU," and then Victor went outside *and fed her cocktail peanuts* and I was like, "YOU ARE REWARDING BAD BEHAVIOR," and he was all, "*But she's hungry,*" and I was pretty sure we'd just switched bodies.

I tossed the traps but I found a big plastic owl that's supposed to scare away rodents and Victor was like, "We're not buying a Big Al," and I said, "Well, we have to now because you just named it Big Al." And he was like, "I said '*big owl,*'" and I said, "Well good, because that's a *terrible* name and a waste of an owl. We should name it Hootie. Or Owl Roker. Or . . . OWLEXANDER HAMILTON."

We brought Owlexander Hamilton home but I felt bad about leaving him outside at night and Victor was like, "WHY IS A PLASTIC OWL IN OUR BED?" and I explained that the directions said,

Hoot hoot, motherfucker.

"Must be moved to different locations for maximum efficiency," and Victor glared at me so I claimed innocence and told him the owl probably did it himself. "He's like Hootini." And Victor just shook his head and said, "I'm talon you, this has to stop." And moments like this are why we're still married.

Hey, remember how this chapter started off ten years ago about solar eclipses and I got sidetracked by rodents? WTF, me. Get your shit together.

I didn't want to go buy a welding helmet because the hardware store people kept judging me about lawn gerbils, but I found a website that explained how you could make a solar eclipse viewer by putting a cardboard box on your head and poking a small pinhole through the back, allowing the eclipse to project in the front of the box. It seemed ridiculous but I did it and it totally worked. And by "it totally worked" I mean that I spent ten minutes standing in the front yard with a box on my head as I stared at the small, unchanging white sun spot that ended up actually being a fleck of Styrofoam stuck to the inside of the box.

I tried it again but I kept losing my balance and eventually fell in the rat bushes, and when I took off the box I noticed that a neighbor had slowed down his truck in front of my house and was just watching me stagger around the yard with a box on my head, so I

loudly explained, "IT"S SO I WON"T STARE AT THE SUN." He
nodded and drove away and then I thought that I probably should
have explained that there was an eclipse but at that point it was too
late, so instead I just went in to have a cocktail and toasted to the
never-ending horror that is nature.

Business Ideas to Pitch on *Shark Tank*

There's a show on TV called *Shark Tank* where people pitch their ideas in campy infomercial style to millionaire venture capitalists in hopes that they will invest in their inventions. I was contacted by one of the people who work on *Shark Tank* to see if I wanted to write about some of their more successful products but that sounded really boring, so instead I asked if I could come on the show with some of my friends to pitch our product. We didn't actually have a product at the time but Victor and I brainstormed with our friends (and several bottles of rum) and we came up with a series of incredibly inappropriate products and pitches that we thought would be great for the show. We decided to come up with lots of ideas so that if the Sharks looked skeptical we could just quickly jump to the next one, like we were contestants on *Super Password*. We even brainstormed names for a parent company that would manage all of these subsidiaries. I liked the name We Shouldn't Sue Them Corporation because whenever people discussed us they'd automatically be subconsciously defending us, but in the end we decided that getting the Sharks on board was more important, so we narrowed it down to YoudBeARealAssholeNotToInvest.com and LetsGetArrestedTOGETHER.org.

The next morning we sobered up and read the pitches I'd emailed to *Shark Tank* and realized I'd probably never get a reply back. Mostly because these ideas were fucking brilliant and we'd given them away for free rather than applying for patents.

Since the ideas were so strong, I'm including them in my book so that if one of the Sharks "suddenly" starts selling a placenta dehydrator I can say, "Nuh-uh, motherfucker. NOT ON MY WATCH. You done fucked up, because that shit is ours."

Here are a few of our ideas (maybe skip this chapter if you're under seventeen, okay?):

Idea 1: Sandal Spats: Spats to wear over flip-flops, so you're fancy even at the pool. Think "Mr. Peanut goes to the beach." (Also, great title for a movie. Movie rights available. Maybe.)

Idea 2: The Affirmator: An affirmative vibrator designed to counter the shame of masturbation. Masturbation that's so good for you even the Pope might recommend it. It has a programmable electronic voice box, which says positive affirmations like "It's okay. Everyone does it. Your hair looks fantastic today, by the way. *Down there* [*raises eyebrow*]." It'd be like you're fucking Stephen Hawking (might mispronounce names though) and it can tweet out how active you are. Also, it has a pedometer so you can count calories, which lets you feel like you're doing something healthy. We were going to call it the Pedomator but we were concerned it might sound like we were affirming pedophilia. *We're not for that.*

Idea 3: The Placenta Tote: Like a DivaCup but bigger, for people who like to hoard their blood. And it comes with accessories like the Placenta Dehydrator. "Long flight? No worries! Make your own snacks! Full of iron! Backpacking through the Klondike? Feed everyone! Watch out for bears though." Another great thing is that vegans can eat it too because no one had to die to make it and it doesn't have a face. We can sell placenta rubs and marinades because **you're gonna need spices.** *Trust me on this one.* You *will* need the spices. Or use our patented Placenta Injector if it's too dry. Bonus: No one will ever ask for your jerky. It's all for you. (We could also just sell the Placenta Tote to keep your regular jerky in so that no one ever tries to take your snacks.)

Idea 4: The Devo Cup: For when you don't want to swallow. No cleanup necessary. Just attach the Devo Cup at the moment of ejaculation. Slogan: "Make your little buddy look like a member of Devo and put on a concert!" (PS: Get permission from Devo first.)

Idea 5: Genital crabs with glitter stuck to them so that when they move around they catch the light like a disco ball of Swarovski crystals, but made of bugs. We'll call them Fancy Crabs! Possible slogan: "Fancy Crabs! It's a disco in your pants!" Plus, Fancy Crabs will spread to your partner and then they can't cheat on you without revealing to others that they are taken because if the crabs don't stick, the glitter sure fucking will. Seriously, glitter is **way** harder to get rid of than crabs. Not that I'd know. I don't have glitter.

Idea 6: Rapid Raccoon Retrievals. We find wild raccoons and we teach them to collect golf balls so we can sell them back to golf courses. We just let them loose and they'll fill their fanny packs with balls (we have to get them fanny packs) and reward them with cat food or tiny hats or whatever it is raccoons want. And also you teach them to retrieve spare change. And foldin' money. And then you let them loose in the mall. Sure, they might occasionally mug a few people, but it's totally worth the story. "I was just paying for my corn dog and a motherfucking raccoon **burgled me**." That is one to tell the grandkids, my friends. They can also jump in the mall fountains and pull out quarters and sneak into cars in car washes. They jump in and steal all the change for tolls, and they have naturally tiny hands to reach under seats. Our *Shark Tank* presentation would go like this: "Talk about a growing problem . . . aimless, marauding packs of raccoons with no career training or opportunities. We will educate them, give them jobs, and make them important members of society. We're seeking two million dollars for twenty percent of what our best raccoon brings in." It's basically like prostitution but cuter.

And if the raccoons get sick we can change it to Rabid Raccoon Retrieval so we could still use the same monogram, and also even the sick raccoons would still probably bring you stuff, but rabies makes you loopy so truthfully you don't know what you're going to get back. Rabies, probably.

Our slogan: "Solutions. With Raccoons."

Idea 7: Jean Sleeves. An ecological fashion line of clothes repurposed in creative ways. Socks can be male thongs. Leg warmers can be scarves that make your neck look thinner. Shoes filled with cotton make earmuffs. Slogan: "Jean Sleeves. Buy them. For your arms. You think they're pants . . . but they're not. They're for your arms." We will make a million dollars selling this stuff. Except that no one needs to buy this stuff since they already have all of it. Damn it. This one needs a rethink.

Idea 8: Dick Dazzler: (A BeDazzler, but for dicks.) Tiny penis? All nest and no bird? From the makers of Mangina Pro comes the new Dick Dazzler. Tired of branding your dick? Tried drawing on it to make it noticeable? Try something more permanent. Dick Dazzler! Have a mighty falcon between your legs through our patented use of applied prisms and rhinestones and illusions. Act now and get our unique Taint Painter, sure to make your brown eye blue. It's taintastic! Coming soon: Taintanium (the gold-leaf version).

Idea 9: From the makers of Dick Dazzler comes Cock Pocket! It's a pocket made from your own foreskin. (We can just use the Hot Pocket jingle because it's super catchy.) Cock Pocket! Looking for something less permanent? Try Crotch Crochet! Finally you can combine your love of crocheting with your enormous pubic bush and crochet your briar patch into a penis purse. Make a rucksack for your man sack. It's macramé for men. *Mancramé.*

Idea 10: From the makers of Crotch Crochet comes Diamonique Mittens (bath mittens with rhinestones BeDazzled all

over them) for fancy hand jobs. It exfoliates . . . sexily. SO
ELEGANT!

Commercial: Wife giving a hand job brags about saving fifty
   cents buying the generic version of Diamonique Mittens. She
   looks to her husband for praise but he looks pained. Puzzled,
   she looks at her Diamonique Mittens, which are now bloody.
Her: Oh no. All I've got is skin.
Husband: What have you done, Karen? You've hit the bone.
Her (to the camera): Uh-oh. I did it again! Help us, Mangina
   Pro!
Announcer: Don't let this happen to you! Use only real Diamonique Mittens. Accept no substitutes. Substitutes are made
   with razor blades and hepatitis. Or so we've heard. Act now
   and get our patented salted-lemon massage cream!
Happy wife: So much better! Jazz hands!
Husband: Honey, I think you mean "jizz hands"!
(Both laugh.)
Announcer: Gross high five, you guys! Visit HandJobFancy
   .com today! Single mittens available for a hip Michael Jackson look. Or for people missing a hand. Or people with
   an extra hand. Whatever. We don't discriminate. Get your
   freak on, ya weirdos.

Idea 11: Guys love fancy shaving brushes, so let's step it up.
My Shaving Brush is made of the cock hairs of a unicorn. Our
Shark would have to source the unicorns but the idea is that
you find the unicorns and pluck their cocks. Lots of them.
It's like high-thread-count sheets. Watch out. They're bitey if
they're anything like donkeys. (Don't ask.)

Idea 12: Stilts are great to help you hang curtains, but what if your curtains are on the second floor? Get a little help from Pogo Stilts. All the stability of stilts with the added random height of a pogo stick. Slogan: "Pogo Stilts: Someone's breaking a leg!"

Idea 13: The My Buddy app. Make yourself feel better by comparison by using the My Buddy app to pair yourself with someone in your area who will come to parties and behave worse than you so you feel less awful. Did you just drunkenly tell an off-color joke to a group of people who are now glaring at you? Call your buddy and he'll say something way more horrific. He'll just walk in and say, "Did you know the Holocaust wasn't real?" or "I think eating babies is totes underrated." Rate whatever terrible thing you said on a scale from 1 to 5 and you'll be matched with a buddy in your area. Additionally you can blame all the terrible things you said on being a buddy.

We can also use the My Nemesis app. Use an arrow to point to people you want to fuck with and strangers have to say stuff like, "I can't believe you beat that assault charge. You're drinking again?" Or "Remember last night when you were trying to blow yourself and I had to stop you before you got cramps again? Take it easy tonight. How's your rash?"

(We can use the My Buddy doll's theme song. Everyone wins. Unless we get sued by the people who made My Buddy. But if they try to sue us we'll just call our buddy and he'll come up with something worse so we can both be mad at him.)

Idea 14: From the makers of Sandal Spats comes Sandal Spurs! Great for if you want to ride a horse in your flip-flops.

(We're still in the R & D stage on this one but it's gonna be huge.)

Idea 15: When hairless cats curl up into a ball, their excess belly skin looks a lot like a lady garden, so we can have the best of both worlds by adopting unwanted hairless cats and using them for photo shoots of "vaginas" so that we can make a Pornhub that doesn't exploit actual women. We'll call it "bald pusses" and technically we can't get sued for lying.

Idea 16: Signature fragrances are big right now but they all smell the same, so now is the time to market a smell that really sums up the year. Something like the tangy musk of desperation and broken plumbing. Add a note of fear. Name ideas: Flea Market Man-Juice, Carnie Musk, Hobo Stench, Haunted Trucker, Backwoods Banjo Wood Chipper, Gluten-Free Possum (because people really like gluten-free stuff nowadays), Caged Stank: Call of the Feral Porcupine, Horse Rape. (Probably not the last one but I'm leaving it on in case the other ones are already taken.) Slogan: "Don't spray it on your privates unless you want to get pregnant."

Idea 17: Here's a question: What do people like even better than cocaine? Fried food. And what do they like even more than fried food? Sticks. You know what no one has ever thought of? Fried cocaine on a stick. Y'all, *we're gonna be zillionaires.*

Idea 18: Create a show called *Science Fair Crashers*. Break into science fairs and see if people will fall for terrible science projects that we make. Episode ideas: "Is this acid or water?" "Taste test. Which is better? You chose human baby. Don't get mad at me. You ate the baby. It's not even grass-fed or local." "Antifreeze or Kool-Aid?" "Does anthrax have a smell?" "Can people identify semen just by taste?"

Idea 19: Milk bars are hot right now but they never go anywhere. How about a food truck that only has one live cow in it who will squirt raw milk right into your open maw? Like Meals on Wheels but better. Teats on the Streets. Street Teats. It sings.

Idea 20: Stop the illegal drug epidemic by adding crap to drugs so people won't think they're cool anymore. Like, cut heroin with powdered milk. That way people who are lactose intolerant will think heroin gives them explosive diarrhea. Also, a series of antidrug commercials of me shitting myself. Because you know what doesn't seem cool? A middle-aged woman shitting herself.

Idea 21: From the makers of Sandal Spats and Sandal Spurs comes Sandal Splats, disposable spats to wear when you have to go to the bathroom on the side of the road. "Keep your shoes safe from pee splashes or diarrhea splash-back with Sandal Splats!"

Idea 22: We are currently in an environmental crisis as islands of floating garbage pile up in our oceans. Reclaim and recycle with Repurposed Cocks (.com). Go carbon neutral using discarded dildos as neck rests on planes, foot rollers for arthritis, blackjacks for self-defense, dog chews, or very short bungee cords. Repel rubber bullets (note: test this first), use them as dog toys for fetching, or stuff in cribs for baby bumpers that double as teethers. (Wash first.)

Idea 23: Scrotal Suspenders for old men. No explanation needed.

Strange New Weather Patterns

It won't always be like this.

I say this to myself over and over.

It runs through my head and if I say it enough I can almost drown out the other voices . . . the ones telling me I'm worthless. The ones telling me that the paralysis I've had in my mind will never end. The ones that lie and wheedle and sometimes tell the truth just enough to make you listen and wonder if they're right. The ones that hurt and bite and sound exactly like me but more confident.

It won't always be like this.

It's true.

I know it will get better. I've seen the dozens of notes I've written to myself in the past. Ones where I say that the sun has come back up and I can breathe and see and feel. It's like coming out of being underwater for too long. That first breath is so perfect, and I just have to hold on because it will happen again and it is so, so good. I read messages from past me saying to keep strong and stay around because once the light is here again I will know entirely that the lies depression tells are just that . . . lies. I promise myself that it's worth it. Or, rather, the person that I was promises the person that I am that it's worth it. And I trust her, a little, and doubt her a little. She is not entirely reliable. She's crazy and unstable. But she's also truthful. So I hold on and wait. And then, eventually, out of nowhere, it comes.

It won't always be like this.

It's true.

And it's a promise I make to myself. But it's also a warning.

The light is bright on those good days. I can feel fully . . . both good and bad. I laugh and cry. I have energy to live. I can see the world and let the world see me with eyes that don't hurt. I see my daughter. I see my friends and family and I feel how lucky I am.

Sometimes it's a promise. Sometimes it's a warning. A warning that the good moments need to be appreciated. That dark comes too . . . just as light does. I embrace the moments when life is good and strong and grab on to the light without apology. Brighter days are coming.

Last night it snowed.

That might not seem like much to you but snow is rare here. Rare as diamonds and—in my opinion—more beautiful. The newsman said it's the first real snowfall here in thirty years and I can believe it. It seemed like everyone in Texas was outside last night, marveling at the soft white flakes that melted on the hot asphalt but managed to survive on the trees and grass and patio chairs. There were family snowball fights at midnight between kids who'd never seen snow and parents who knew that sleep on a school night was well worth missing for such a rare event.

And in the morning the snow was still there. Only an inch or so, and patchy, but beautiful. And we all stared at our houses anew and in awe, as if decorator elves had come in the middle of the night to repaint everything we thought we knew. We were trapped in driveways by tree limbs heavy with snow that suddenly sagged and blocked our way. We were baffled when the car wipers wouldn't push the snow off the windshields and we searched like terrible MacGyvers to find tools to brush it all off. (I used a stuffed monkey puppet and a plunger. My neighbor used a leaf blower and a yardstick. We were about as successful as you would imagine.)

Dorothy Barker whines at the door to be let out, but it's a hesitant whine. One in spite of herself. It's drizzling now and she hates the rain so she must really need to go.

We stand under an umbrella outside and she looks miserable but she pushes forward into the patches of snow that are still left. She smells the place she always smells and for the first time I see the animal tracks left in the snow. Deer, I think. Or foxen. Small feet. And suddenly I can see the world she smells, and how she puts together stories with her nose that are only revealed to me through snow. She looks at me as if to say, *See. I told you.* I nod. She wins.

I notice something so strange . . . the rain continues but the streets shine with bright sunlight. I walk out into the street and close my umbrella. There's no rain there. I can't understand it at first and I look all around me until I'm certain of it.

The trees are raining.

The trees are raining and I don't understand. But then I do. The new snow in the leaves is melting so quickly it's created a downpour. I stand in the street with my dog and we watch the rain come down all around us while we feel the warming sun. My neighbor says it's like being under God's protection. I say it's like being Storm from X-Men. Dorothy Barker says nothing because she's a dog, and anyway I suspect dogs are used to feeling like God-blessed superheroes.

If I lived up north this would probably feel normal. If I lived up north I would probably not have driven all over my neighborhood to see the places I don't even really *see* anymore transformed by the snow. If I lived up north I would have probably thought the people stopping their cars in the middle of the road to take pictures of white-topped bushes were crazy. We were all crazy, and we knew it could not last.

But I didn't expect this. This second weather phenomenon. I didn't expect the trees to become storm clouds. I've been alive for more than forty years and I've never seen this . . . I've never seen trees rain.

I whisper, *It makes me wonder what else I haven't seen yet.*

You haven't seen the foxen, Dorothy Barker seems to say (with a little more superiority than necessary if I'm being honest).

It's true though. It's a nice reminder. There are things I haven't seen yet.

It's time to get busy.

Souls

I'm not much for organized religion, but I think we all have souls.

Glowing half orbs. Flat at our back and round at our chests, like glass paperweights with golden candy-button dots at the center. And as we live, our spheres crack. They splinter with sadness or loss or doubt or pain. Sometimes the splinter that falls out is a loss of faith. Sometimes it's the loss of love or a betrayal. Sometimes it's just a lack of structural integrity (depression/chemical issues) that causes irregular shards to fall out. Then we walk around with these slivers missing . . . these holes. We try to put the slivers back in place, but they don't fit right anymore and so we leave them. And then we search.

Sometimes we find a tiny piece that fills a hole incompletely but helps to fill the gap. Sometimes it's a song that speaks important words we couldn't form ourselves. Sometimes it's a line of truth from a book. We pick it up and take it into ourselves and it fits. It stops up the hole. The crack is still there but it's a small fissure that's only noticeable to ourselves or the people we let close enough to feel our imperfect spheres.

Sometimes we try to fill these holes with things that seem to fill the gap but aren't right. We wedge a square bit in a round hole, but it's a large hole, so it fits, although inexactly. It feels okay for a bit but it keeps the truly healing splinters from being taken inside. It blocks the things you really need. Maybe that square shape you can't let go of is alcohol or drugs. Maybe it's comfort found in the wrong place or with the wrong person. Maybe it's a job that you take to fill the gap instead of finding the passion you need because you can't live with a gaping hole in your chest. Because the hole leads to a fragile place. A place you can't protect. A place that can be destroyed, the core of which is meaningless once the light goes out (even if it's now protected by the put-back-together pieces) because in the time it was open it was too badly damaged, or squandered, or taken. It sometimes happens after abuse or trauma, or in people who have a terrible wall up and no soft core inside to find compassion, or to feel love, or to trust. And the only way to get yourself out of this hell is to break your sphere apart and leave yourself open to healing. It's an exercise in trust, because that can't just come from you. It comes from love. From family, or friends, or compassionate strangers, or faith, or therapy, or the trust of a small child or sweet animal.

Sometimes the sphere is too broken for people to go on. It's like when people say their God hole is empty. We're all built differently, and maybe for you the missing piece is religion or trust or love or acceptance, but we're all shattered in our own way and we all pick up pieces that others leave behind. Sometimes those pieces are people— people who've been rejected and left discarded as trash because they didn't fit for someone else, but they fit perfectly with you.

Sometimes the holes line up and you can lean into someone

else's emptiness and block out the empty for a bit, but that doesn't last forever. Codependence never does.

Sometimes the people you love leave you even when they don't want to and you shatter into pieces. You may not be able to find all of those pieces again because when they left they took a few with them. It hurts, but the pain eventually becomes bearable and even sacred because it's how you carry the people you've lost with you. And if you're lucky you can one day see that the hollow spots you carry are in the shape of their face or their hands or the love they gave you. Those holes ache, but they are a monument to the lost, a traveling sacred place to honor them and remind you of how to love enough to leave your own marks on others.

Sometimes your sphere grows and swells almost painfully when you see something that brings back your faith in humanity and in yourself. Sometimes you see your child and your chest swells so much that it makes the holes smaller. Sometimes the pieces you lost when you were young come back to you, in a remembered hum of a lullaby or a piece of wisdom that you couldn't accept at the time because it didn't fit . . . but it fits now, because it fits the you that you've become.

Sometimes you can pull out shards from your own chest to give to others, but done indiscriminately it leaves a void in you, because if they're given too easily and haphazardly they won't fit the person you've given them to and will be lost to you both. You learn early that you don't always get a shard back in return. That's a good lesson though, because it reminds you of your worth and of the worth of the shards that fit.

Some people blithely leave shards as they go along in the world, dropping love and art and kindness and inspiration and the healing message that *YOU ARE NOT ALONE*, and that sadness is sometimes okay, and that joy will come again and again even if you're not sure what it looks like. Those people make magic words and bittersweet songs and raucous art and beautiful pain. Those people make the world go around.

Others walk with sledgehammers, smashing spheres and leaving the shards behind, unaware of their value, and sometimes even doubting their existence. Their footsteps crunch past us and we try to remember that things could be worse . . . that we could be them, dark and shattered and numb. Because pain is bad, but numb is a thing too terrible for words. We scream and attack the sledgehammer wielders. Or we avoid their eyes and pray for them to not see us. Or we weep for them and try to put them back together. It doesn't always work . . . but when it does, it's blinding.

And some people, like me, have a shard forever missing, a chasm that goes straight down to the core. Anxiety. It creates a fear—of people, of strangers and friends, and of life. It makes you fragile and vulnerable and you throw up walls so that no one can reach inside, because you have to protect that core.

But—and here's the tricky part—*you also have to protect the break* . . . that empty place that you always feel, because that break is what makes you who you are.

My therapist says I'm too empathetic for my own good. That I pick up on other people's emotions and feelings and then I feel them myself even when it hurts. And she's right. That's why I have to separate myself from others, from even life sometimes . . . to keep safe the soft core that shines when I find people like me . . . who are good but broken. Who want nothing but happiness. Who would give you their shoes, or their stories, or sometimes even their own precious, collected shards. The shards that they've worked for, and love, and treasure. And sometimes they do give them. And sometimes you give them back some of yours. And you're surprised to find that these shards fit better.

Sometimes you pick up the shards that others no longer need, the ones that are so healthy and strong that they grow too large to use and they discard them like tree bark or snakeskin. And then you pull them into yourself because what these people grow is what you need. And then *you* grow, and push out shards of your own for others who follow behind you.

The world is shattered and we wander barefoot through one another's broken shards and glittering slivers. And some of us bleed from the cuts. And some of us heal. And if you're lucky, you do both.

We are broken. We are healing. It never ends.

And, if you look at it in just the right light, it is beautiful.

A Note about the Cover

Once, several years ago, I came across a painting of a child lovingly holding a grotesque but fascinating sort of demon monster. She seemed perfectly content, and held the creature as if it was a giant beloved dog. I looked up the artist (Omar Rayyan) and found his strange and whimsical paintings of people carrying their own baffling little monsters, dangerous-looking creatures that were wild and untamed and often happily destroying everything around them. I suspect I'm projecting, but I've never seen a collection of art that more perfectly encapsulated how I felt about my own battle with depression and anxiety and the monsters in my head.

My personal beasties are ugly and ridiculous and they weigh me down and are exhausting to carry around. Sometimes it feels like they are larger than I am. They are destructive and baffling and ungainly.

And yet.

And yet, there is something wonderful in embracing the peculiar and extraordinary monsters that make us unique. There is joy in accepting the curious and erratic beasts that force us to see the world in new ways. And there is an uncanny sort of fellowship that comes when you recognize the beasties that other people carry with them and the battles we are all fighting even when they seem invisible to the rest of the world.

We all have these monsters, I suspect, although they come from different places and have different names and causes. But what we do with them makes a difference. And, whenever I can, I take mine out in the sun and try to appreciate that the flowers it rips up from the garden can sometimes be just as lovely when stuck in the teeth of its terrible mouth.

Embrace your beasties. Love your awkwardness. Enjoy yourself. Celebrate the bizarreness that is you because, I assure you, you are more wondrous than you can possibly imagine . . . monsters and all.

Acknowledgments

Whenever I write acknowledgments I always feel conflicted because what if people hate this book and they're burning it and then in the acknowledgments I'm like, "THANK YOU TO THIS SPECIFIC PERSON WITHOUT WHOM THIS WOULD NOT EXIST," and then they're like, "I HAD NOTHING TO DO WITH THIS BOOK. JESUS. I DON'T EVEN KNOW HER, Y'ALL."

Also, I don't like the word "acknowledgments" because it sounds like you were forced to thank people against your will. We should change it to "Thank-yous" or "THESE FUCKERS." Oh, I like that one.

THESE FUCKERS

I would like to thank a lot of amazing people because without these fuckers none of this would be possible.

Thank you to my family for giving me such amazing stories and allowing me to write them. Thank you to Victor and Hailey for making me laugh. Thank you to my parents for always laughing with me. And at me. Both, really.

Thank you to my agent, Neeti Madan, who is made of stardust, and my editor, Amy Einhorn, who is made of magic. I'm so sorry every book of mine takes three years longer than expected. Thank you to Conor and Maggie and Marian and Pat and Caitlin and Allison and Maia and Jason and Chris and Michelle and Vincent and Aja and Hannah and Matie and Matt and a million other people on the team who have helped in ways you cannot possibly imagine. Thank you to Omar Rayyan for painting this incredible cover and to Denise Kendig for drawing me so well I wanted to stamp my picture on every copy of this book (and so I did).

Thank you to my friends for letting me read the same chapters to you over and over and over again. Maile, Laura, Karen, Lisa, Stephen . . . you are saints.

Thank you to Maile and Jason for late nights of drinking that inspired ridiculousness that is so inappropriate that I will not use your last names here to protect you.

Thank you to the doctors and nurses and therapists who saved me. And continue to save me.

Thank you to book reviewers and buyers and supporters and sellers and people who smile at random dogs on the street.

Thank you to the people who let me share their words and inspired mine.

Thank you to the person I forgot to mention here but who is so understanding that they forgive me and will write their name in themselves. I love you the most, _____.

And thank you to you. Yes, *you*. The person reading this. You are the reason this book exists. So if you hate it I guess you sort of have to blame yourself.

Thank you for listening. Really. I super crazy love you. No hyperbole.

About the Author

Jenny Lawson, the Bloggess, is a humor writer known for her candor in addressing her struggle with depression and mental illness. Her first book, *Let's Pretend This Never Happened*, debuted at number one on the *New York Times* bestseller list, and her second book, *Furiously Happy*, spent five months on the *New York Times* bestseller list.